GEOGRAPHY

COURSEWORK COMPANION

Norman Law

GCSE

Charles Letts & Co Ltd
London, Edinburgh & New York

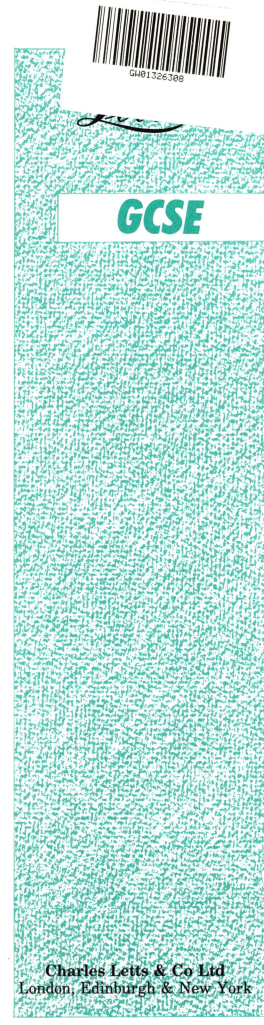

First published 1989
by Charles Letts & Co Ltd
Diary House, Borough Road, London SE1 1DW

Text: © Norman Law 1989
Cover photograph: Steven Hunt, Image Bank
Handwriting samples: Artistic License
Diagrams: Peter McClure
Cartoons: Viv Quillin
Photograph on page 36: Aerofilms Limited
All other photographs supplied by the author
Illustrations: © Charles Letts & Co Ltd 1989

British Library Cataloguing in Publication Data

Law, N. E. (Norman Ernest), *1947–*
  GCSE geography–(Letts coursework
  companion)
  1. Geography–For schools
  I. Title
  910

ISBN 0 85097 860 2

Printed and bound in Great Britain by
Charles Letts (Scotland) Ltd

Contents

Introduction

Try to picture a room full of examination candidates. Their desks are decorated with fluffy animals and good luck charms. The candidates sit anxiously, worried looks on their faces, hoping that the 'right' questions come up in the exam. Everything rests on the next hour or so!

The GCSE was introduced so that you would be more fairly treated than this. No longer would you need a mascot to ensure good luck in the examination. Up to 60 per cent of the marks in geography examinations (depending on syllabus) can now be gained from coursework, as shown in Appendix 1. Believe it or not, the GCSE examiners are on your side. You are now encouraged to show what you have learned, can understand and can do. In simple terms, this means that you will be given credit for your effort and achievement. Everything in the GCSE course is aimed at showing your **positive achievement**, so do not worry about minor errors; we all make them! This book is intended to help you make positive achievements. If you refer to it during your course, it will help you to understand what you are being asked to do. It will also give you useful hints about how to improve your skills. By using this book you will be able to show just what you have achieved and you will be able to improve your grades as a result.

The book is essentially **practical**. It gives you actual examples wherever possible and gives clear hints to follow in your coursework. If you follow the advice given, it will do far more for you than any number of lucky mascots or good luck cards. If you work through it wisely, it will help you to make your own good luck and prove to everyone just how good you are! Let us first look at what the GCSE course will be testing.

General guidance – What the course will test

Your teacher may have given you a copy of your GCSE syllabus. If not, you should find out from your teacher exactly which examination group is operating your examination and which specific syllabus you are studying. You can then send for one by using their address from the list given at the end of this section. There may be a small charge but the syllabus *is* very important.

At the beginning of your syllabus booklet, you will find a list of **assessment objectives**. These set out what you will be expected to be able to do by the end of the course. The objectives are divided into three groups and cover **knowledge and understanding**, **skills** and **values**. These are given different importance (weighting) in different syllabuses, but they must *all* be tested. The weighting in the different syllabuses as far as coursework is concerned is shown in Appendix 1. The meanings of each of the terms and what they cover are described below.

Knowledge and understanding

Knowledge refers to the **facts**, **terms** and **ideas** that you have learned during the course. For example, London has a well-defined pattern of land use within it (the fact). This is known as urban morphology (the term) and there are different theories about how the pattern is arranged (the idea or model).

Understanding means that you should be able to **apply** ideas that you have learnt from one example to the case of another. This application of knowledge is very important in geography. For example, if you have

Table 1.1 Skills and techniques for assessment

Skills	Techniques related to the skills (ways in which the skills could be tested)
Skills of investigation: Organizing and carrying out an investigation showing personal initiative	**Fieldwork investigations:** Data collection techniques including planning ahead and recording data
Communication skills (inc. practical skills): Presenting information clearly using the relevant technique (either verbal, written or in drawn form)	**Verbal (speaking up):** Discussion, role play, decision-making, answering questions verbally **Written:** Writing answers to examination questions, producing written coursework, extended answer writing **Drawing:** Ways of showing data in visual form e.g. graphs, maps, diagrams, tables (see Section Four)
Skills of interpretation: Analysing, interpreting and using data from different sources	**Verbal (reasoning):** Understanding and reacting to points made in debates or discussions **Written:** Written interpretation of all sorts of documents, including books, photos, maps and diagrams, e.g. scatter graphs, isopleths and OS maps **Drawing:** Production of simplified sketch maps and diagrams to show patterns in more complicated material
Skills of evaluation: Looking at the evidence, drawing conclusions from it and making reasoned and balanced judgments	**Making up your mind:** Discussion, debate, decision-making and role play, evaluation of written evidence
Conceptualizing skills: Thinking about the topic and coming out with models and generalizations	**Using models:** Classifying data, applying the understanding drawn from one example to the study of another
Hypothesizing skills: (Using statements which can be tested, leading to prediction, assessment of trends and the use of evidence to make judgments)	**Testing ideas:** Discussion, role play, decision-making, research and investigation

Hints on improving your performance in each of these skills are given in Section Three.

learnt about the internal layout of London, then you should be able to apply the explanations for that layout in the case of Manchester or Bogotá. It also means that you should understand the **process** by which something has come about. For example, it could mean that you look at the stages by which the segregation of land uses in a town has come about. The sequence of development (*stages*) of a landform and why they have happened is another example.

Skills

When people refer to 'skills', they are usually talking about practical skills, such as being able to draw maps and diagrams. Although these are certainly skills, and very important ones, the GCSE examination recognizes that there are many more types than this. Relevant skills are shown in Table 1.1 together with how each may be tested in your coursework. Most GCSE syllabuses make it quite clear which skills are being tested. You should refer to your syllabus booklet if you are in any doubt.

Values

A new feature of the GCSE examination is that it allows you to study people's reactions to geographical developments and to put forward your own feelings on the matter. You are encouraged to comment on what you think about various issues, using information from a wide variety of sources. People's values are often very important in decisions they make. At times, people can make decisions which *look* quite illogical but these are probably made as a result of the **values** they place on the information they have.

Coursework

In the past, subjects were mainly examined by various tests at the end of the course. These tests, or 'examinations' as they are known, put pressure on candidates to remember large amounts of material. For those who were ill, possibly suffering from hayfever for example, such examinations were unfair. The fact that everything rested on the candidate's performance for an hour or two made many people question their fairness.

This is one of the reasons for the introduction of the GCSE examination, with its emphasis on coursework. This is commonly known as **continuous assessment**. As shown in Appendix 1, coursework marks now count for between 20 and 60 per cent of the overall total for the subject. They can be achieved by having to answer in a number of different styles of assessment, which are also listed per syllabus in Appendix 1. Each of the possible types is also listed below, together with a short explanation of what it entails. Check which syllabus you are studying, look at Appendix 1 to see what sorts of coursework you will be expected to submit and then refer to the list below to see which sorts apply to you. Hints on how to approach each type are given later in the book.

Types of coursework assessment

There are several styles of work which could be used in coursework assessments. Some assessments may be like the 'old' examination, where having completed a section of work, you will be given a series of questions and expected to answer them using what you have learnt. This style is unlikely to form the whole of one assessment, but may form part of one.

An assessment is more likely to be an integral part of your course. For instance, you might have learnt about city life in the Developing World by studying São Paulo. To widen your experience, as well as testing whether you have understood the main ideas involved with the topic, you might be asked to study another Developing World city, such as Bogotá. Such a coursework assessment would be a teaching unit *as well as* being designed to find out what you have learnt about cities in the Developing World in general. You would probably be given the question sheet and asked to hand in your answers about two weeks later. This means that you will have every opportunity to look at atlases, discuss things with other people, refer to books in the library and carefully check your work before handing it in.

In addition, coursework assessments could contain . . .

You will have plenty of time to prepare for assessments. Make sure you use the time wisely.

Oral assessments

You might be asked a series of questions and be expected to give your answers by speaking to your teacher. You might also be asked to talk about something you have studied by yourself. This would give you an opportunity to prove that you have understood the example without having to bother about spelling or grammar!

Debates and role play

As part of a coursework assessment, you might also have to debate a topic. Sometimes you are asked to pretend to be somebody in such a debate. You might, for example, be given the role of a government minister in a debate on the location of a new power station. You would be expected to read some background information about the person and the proposal and then speak about the subject as you think that minister would.

Teacher-planned enquiries

Sometimes you might be directed by your teacher to carry out some fieldwork. This could be to investigate a problem, such as the flow of traffic in an area. Your teacher would tell you what the problem is, how you are going to collect your data and when to do so. After collecting such data, you would be expected to analyse it yourself and answer questions based upon the information. The collection of data in this case would be done by yourself, or in groups, in class time or on fieldwork. Subsequent analysis would probably be done for homework or in class, but working by yourself.

Individual studies

Several of the 'old' examinations required candidates to produce projects. The best ones were where a question was asked as the title and the student had to find a way of investigating the topic, coming up with an answer well supported by facts. The worst ones were where students took a topic such as 'The Rocky Mountains' and copied endless text from library books. In the GCSE, the second type should be avoided **at all costs**. Remember that you are being tested on your geographical ability, not whether you can read and copy from books. The individual study should therefore be based on a question. It should involve your own personal research and come up with a clearly presented and well-supported answer.

Geographical enquiries

This term is used by some examination groups to mean the same as 'Individual Study'. In others, it means a shorter piece of work, perhaps supported by fieldwork. Look in your syllabus document to see exactly what is required of you.

Coursework studies

You might be asked to do some research during your course on a topic you are studying. You might be asked to work on census data for your local area during a study of cities, for example. This work from secondary sources will be well directed for it will involve answering some questions relating to the data provided for you.

Decision-making exercises

Some syllabuses, for example the MEG syllabus C, involve you in responding to data and making a decision based upon it. For example, you might be given a lot of information about three possible routes for a new road. You could be given the views of different people involved in the decision, the costs of the alternatives, information on their environmental impact, and maps or photographs of the area. Working through a series of exercises, you would eventually be expected in this case to decide which route is the best. You would also have to support your decision with reference to the background information you have been given.

Fieldwork

Several of the assessment styles referred to above involve fieldwork. You might in addition be asked to carry out a number of individual fieldwork exercises in order to complete a notebook. This would be submitted as part of your coursework.

Whichever assessment pattern is followed in your syllabus, remember that it is designed to help you! You will not be under pressure to remember everything in an hour or two at the end of the course. However, you will need to plan your time very carefully if you are to do yourself justice in the various types of coursework assessment. The chance is there for you to show what you have learnt, can understand and can do. Be positive – take that chance!

✓ **Checklist 1**

1 Refer to your copy of the syllabus.

2 Check which types of assessment you will be asked to complete.

Planning your work

Organization is the key to GCSE success!

The key to success is **organization**. The GCSE is no exception to this rule. In fact, it requires you to complete a fair amount of work, probably at regular intervals through the course. All of this will be marked as part of your grade, so it requires you to be particularly well organized. There are several things you should do in order to make sure that you complete your work on time and sufficiently well to obtain a good grade. These are outlined below.

General preparation

1 You should make sure that you have the **right equipment**. In geography, the following items are essential. Obviously it is best if they belong to you. If you can't purchase them, make sure that you can easily borrow them, or work somewhere that they are available. Some of the items could form part of a birthday or Christmas present list!

- writing equipment, including pen, soft and hard lead pencils
- 30 cm ruler
- protractor, set square, compasses, dividers
- rubber
- coloured pencils
- atlas (ask your teacher's advice on the best one to buy and make sure it is as up-to-date as possible)
- calculator

2 Get used to completing a **diary** for the work you have to do. You will probably have a homework diary from your school, which you could use for this purpose. This practice will enable you to face up to the challenge of planning coursework assessments much more easily (see below). In the run up to examinations, you could well use a similar technique in the planning of your examination revision. Your school should make sure that you are *not* asked to complete several pieces of coursework for different subjects at the same time. If you *are,* you should certainly talk to your form tutor or teacher. An example of a diary plan for one assessment is shown in Fig. 2.1.

3 Practise the **techniques** you learn during your course. The assessments will test these techniques much more than the facts you have learnt. If you have difficulty with reading Ordnance Survey maps, for example, do not ignore them and hope to be lucky; ask your teacher for help. There are also many guides available. You can find these in your local library or even your school library. If you have trouble drawing maps and diagrams, practise them. Obviously, a major source of help in any of these things is your teacher, but others who might assist are sixth formers, parents and even class friends.

Specific preparation for a coursework assessment

1 When the work is given out, make sure that you understand what you have to do. You **must** ask if you are in any doubt. You could use the following ideas.

a) Read through the material carefully. If you are allowed to write on

Plan

Date	Geography assessment	Other work
Mon 7	Assessment received. Choose type of location by discussing with Mum. Plan data collection sheet.	English homework
Tues 8		Science and maths homework
Wed 9	Visit shopping centre to see where best to carry out the survey.	Home Economics homework
Thurs 10	Collect graph paper from Geog. teacher	History homework
Fri 11		History homework
Sat 12	Collect fieldwork information with Mum.	
Sun 13	Plan and produce diagrams from field data	
Mon 14	Geog. Homework. Begin write up using diagrams.	English homework
Tues 15	(Ask about any problems)	Science and maths homework
Wed 16	Write explanation of pattern	Home Economics homework
Thurs 17		maths homework
Fri 18	Complete Geography Assessment	
Sat 19	Read through work and check.	
Sun 20	A day of rest!	
Mon 21	HAND IT IN !!!!	

Fig. 2.1 A diary plan

Comment:
Notice the time left for checking and the prompt start to the work. See note 4 below.

the question sheet, **underline** any questions you do not understand or terms which you do not know. If you cannot write on the sheet, make a list on a piece of paper.

b) **Ask** your teacher to explain anything of which you are unsure and make a note of the answer. Listen carefully to your teacher's explanations to the questions of other pupils.

c) When you are clear that you know what is required, **highlight** the main things you have to do. For example, you could put a circle around all the **direction** words (such as **write, describe, explain, compare** etc.). You could also underline all the **subjects**, such as **places, areas, people, industries** etc. An example would be:

Describe the site of Sonning village.

d) **Plan** your work, using the highlights you have produced. You should make a grid, possibly with the layout below.

Question	Marks available	Research needed
3a	4	Atlas map of NE Africa

Table 2.1

2 You now have a list of things you need to find out before you can answer all the questions. **Finding the information** should be your next priority. The usual sources are school and local libraries, but do not forget that everyone in your class will be after the same information. For that reason, you should move quickly and as soon as you have finished with it, return it for others! If you cannot find the information you need, **let your teacher know** in good time. Don't leave it until just before the work is due to be handed in! Your teacher will not believe you then! Other sources of information can be local and national newspapers, local government libraries, atlases (which often include a lot of statistics) and maps of all kinds.

3 **Plan** out your work. Lay it out so that:

a) Each of the questions is clearly labelled, and the teacher (examiner) knows what is being answered.

b) There is plenty of space between each separate answer. This may leave room to insert anything missed out at a later stage, but it is principally so that the work looks neat.

c) Crossings out are kept to a minimum.

d) There is space around all maps and diagrams.

e) All illustrative material has a **title** and, if necessary, a **key**. Mention where you got the information (its *source*).

f) **NB** There may be additional requirements in your particular syllabus. The NEA, for instance, says that squared or graph paper should be *avoided* for anything other than graphs.

4 Answer each question using the **mark scheme** as a general guide as to how much to write. For instance, a question worth ten marks demands a longer answer than one worth two marks. This is not to say that each correct point you write down is worth one mark (although it may be, in some cases). Usually, a certain standard of answer has to be reached before you can be given all the available marks. This is discussed later, but for the moment just think of the mark scheme as a general **guide** to the length of your answer.

5 Plan to finish your answer in plenty of time, leaving you time to **check through**, not only for spelling mistakes and missed words, but also for overall sense and whether you have actually answered the questions set.

Making use of the mark scheme

Fig. 2.2 A station marker

> *Always check to see that you have written what you mean.*

When you are given a coursework question sheet, you will notice that it has the marks available for each answer written on it. You should use this as a guide to the detail required in the answer. Here is an example:

Question

a) State the weather conditions shown by the following station marker (Fig. 2.2). (2)

b) Give four possible reasons for the temperature being so low at this place. (4)

(There would probably be a weather map to go with this question.)

As you can see, there are two marks available for the first part. You are not therefore expected to say very much. There are only three elements of the weather shown by the symbol. The number represents the temperature in degrees Celsius. The double circle shows absolute calm (no wind). The open circle in the centre shows that the sky is clear. Since the question says **describe** and not **state**, you should write in sentences, not notes.

Examples of answers which would be given full marks and one out of two are shown below.

Full marks: The station marker shows clear skies, no wind (calm) and a temperature of minus two degrees Celsius.

One mark: No cloud, wind and temp. −2 degrees.

The trouble with the second answer is that it is a statement rather than a description. In abbreviating it, the student has not made it clear whether 'no wind' or 'wind' was meant. However, it is clearly numbered and the facts are basically correct, although not specific enough to be worth full marks. It is really infuriating since the student obviously knows the information, but has expressed it badly. The teacher or examiner cannot read between the lines. If the student means 'no wind' it must be written as such. The answer will be marked as seen.

The second part of the question needs more information. Here are two attempted answers.

Full marks: *(i)* If the sky is clear at night, heat can escape very quickly from the ground. As the sky is clear at the station, this may be why the temperature has gone below freezing point. *(ii)* The air is calm, so the place may be under a high pressure system (anticyclone). This has subsiding air and therefore clear skies. Clear skies allow the heat to escape. *(iii)* The time of year is important. It is most likely to be weather for the late autumn, winter or early spring. There is not much daytime heat to lose at such times. *(iv)* The time of day is also important. Weather such as this would be more likely to occur at night when there is no incoming heat from the sun, rather than during the day.

Two marks: Heat escapes from clear skies. At night, heat is given off and escapes. It might be winter.

In the first case, the writer has given four good reasons for low temperature – time of day, time of year, atmospheric pressure and lack of clouds. Each reason is carefully worded to leave no room for doubt about what is meant.

In the second case, more than one reason is given, but they are general points, not made specific to the question. Heat does not exactly escape *from* clear skies, so there is some inaccuracy of expression.

This example shows that you can judge the amount of information needed by looking at the marks available. It also shows on which parts of the question you should concentrate. Further, it shows the importance of actually answering the question set. The meaning of the *direction word* is very important. Here are some examples, together with their meanings:

- State – express in a few words (possibly not even a sentence)
- Describe – show the main features of . . .
- Explain, account for – give reasons for . . .

- Compare – show the similarities and differences
- Contrast – show the differences
- Locate – show where it is (often with a map)
- Comment on – give your views on something

✓ Checklist 2 Planning

1 Ensure that you have the right equipment.
2 Plan your work very carefully – use a diary.
3 Practise your techniques as you go.
4 When you are given a piece of coursework:
   a) Read it carefully.
   b) Ask about any problems.
   c) Follow the directions carefully – mark up the question asked.
   d) Plan your answer so that you know what to look for.
   e) Search for the information.
   f) When you write your answer, space it out very carefully.
   g) Label all your answers.
   h) Use the mark scheme as a guide to the length of answer required.
   i) Check through your answer before you hand it in.
5 Make sure that you do what is required by following the *direction word*.

Approaching different types of question

Planning is important, no matter what type of question is involved. Below are three examples of different types of assessment question and how to tackle them.

Structured questions

These are questions, usually linked together by a theme, which lead you gradually through the topic. They often increase in difficulty through the question.

The basic aim of your answer is to put over your ideas as clearly as possible. This means two things:

- It must be well presented.
- It must be logical and not 'padded out'.

The first of these points can be achieved more easily than you think. 'Well presented' does not mean that you have to have good handwriting. As long as you have obviously thought about the layout and space the work out well, you can disguise a lot! The following are two answers to exactly the same question. Spot the differences!

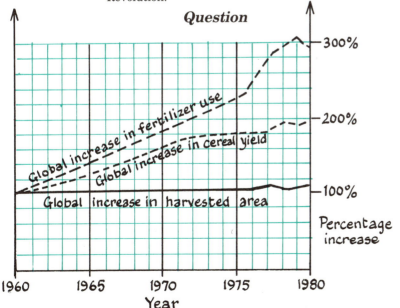

Fig. 2.3 World changes in agriculture due to the Green Revolution.

Question

Refer to Fig. 2.3 which shows some world changes due to the Green Revolution.

a) What is meant by the term 'Green Revolution'? (2)

b) Describe the changes shown in Fig. 2.3. (4)

c) The amount of cereal (wheat, barley etc.) produced, by area, is known as the **yield**. How would the amount of fertilizer used affect the yield of cereals? (3)

d) What other factors, not shown on the graph, could help to explain the yield changes?
Discuss four other factors which might help to explain the changes shown on the graph. (4)

What changes?

Look for pattern and trend, NOT repetition year by year.

1a) or 1b)?

How can fertilizer go up? It was the use which increased. This is read straight from the graph. We need more general descriptions of changes

Untidy!

Cereals can't rise either!

Very interesting, but what about an answer to the last part of the question?

No connection explained

Possible mark:- 5/13

WARNING: COPYING THIS TYPE OF ANSWER CAN SERIOUSLY DAMAGE YOUR CHANCES!

The Green Revolution was a series of farming changes. Fertilizer went up until 1976 when it went up even more until 1977. It reached its highest in 1979 and fell until 1980. By 1979 it was 300% more than in 1960. This helped to explain why cereals rose steadily until 1976. They fell back a little until 1977 and rose again until 1978 but levelled off at just over 200% by 1980. All this time the area of the world being harvested stayed the same. There was no increase in the world's harvested area. Another thing which explained the rise in cereals was new types of plant bred in places such as the International Rice Research Institute in Manila, Philippines. IR8 was one of the new strains of rice produced. It made a great impact on farmers to begin with but was then attacked by various insects to which it was not immune. Many smaller farmers lost all they had because of it. The larger farmers got richer and the smaller ones went out of business.

Fig. 2.4 Answer 1 – Not so good!

In the first answer, the student has not numbered the parts, has paid little attention to the amount required for the different sections and has largely missed the point. The second answer is well spaced out, has enough details and takes note of the number of marks available for each part.

Extended answers

You will probably not be asked to write an essay in geography. An essay is only one form of extended answer, however. Even in writing a paragraph you need to plan carefully. Your answer should be logical and it should apply to actual places or examples rather than being too vague. An example illustrates these points.

Fig. 2.5 Answer 2 – That's better!

1a) In the 1960's and through the 1970's, a number of changes were introduced into farming, especially in parts of the Third World such as South East Asia. These included new crops, new and more vigorous plants, animal breeding, land reform, mechanisation, irrigation and much else. The changes were seen as one way of improving the lives of poor farming families and in some cases they stopped Communist or "Red" Revolutions. They therefore became known as the "Green Revolution".

Dates, examples, location, results and exact reason for term all given.

Well spaced out and clearly numbered.

b) The amount of land available for crops scarcely increased at all between 1960 and 1980, although there was a minor increase around 1978, which came to nothing. During the same period, however, cereal yields increased steadily, with minor fluctuations between 1975 and 1979, to stand at over double the yield in 1980 than there was in 1960. There was an even greater increase in fertilizer use over this period, which ended up around three times as much in 1980 as it had been in 1960. Again, the increase was steady.

Trend

Fluctuation

Rate
Generalised increases ("double" rather than by 200%) Credit for simple maths.

c) Cereal yield increased as fertilizer use increased. ✳ This means that as farmers used the new varieties, which demanded more fertilizer, the amount of artificial fertilizer used also had to increase. An example was the rice crop IR8, which yielded more than four times what some strains of rice had given before, but it only did so if it was well fertilized and watered.

Insert clearly marked.

Connection given first, then explanation not description.

Yield is explained.

* Cereals, especially if grown in a monoculture, are a very demanding crop and only produce a lot of grain (i.e. yield) if they are well cared for.

d) It was not only the use of fertilizers which increased the yield of cereals. Another change was the increase in irrigation. For example, in Rajastan (N.W. India), a large canal has opened up new areas for farming as well as increasing the yield of existing crops. Increased mechanization has increased yields in many areas, for example South East China. When ploughing can be completed quickly, for example, this leaves more time for other farm tasks and improves the chances of increased yield. New seeds have been produced at plant breeding institutes, such as the one at the International Rice Research Institute in Manila, Philippines. These have led to enormous improvements in crop yield so long as irrigation, pesticides and fertilizers are used with them. Better farming methods have also been introduced into areas such as rural Tanzania. These include crop rotation, care of the soil (soil conservation methods), better storage of seeds and the use of appropriate technology for farm implements.

Each statement is backed by an ACTUAL example, which makes it a geographical rather than a general answer

Maximum marks! Note that the length of the answers reflects the marks available.

Question

How and why has the world demand for fuel changed since 1945? (7)
This is the sort of question you could get at the end of a longer question which contains a lot of data, for example graphs, photographs and statistics. You would not be expected to remember all the information. You would be given a lot of hints and asked to answer by referring to them. Table 2.2 is one way of planning the answer.

Change in demand	Reasons	Example
1 Rise	Population, transport, trade increase Growth of towns	Building of motorways
2 Change in type of fuel Coal to oil Oil to others Nuclear Alternatives	Change in technology Cost increases in 1970s Technological change Concern for environment	Trains Power stations France Carmarthen Bay (wind power)

Table 2.2

If you plan your answer like this, you will not forget important elements. You should now be able to use this plan to write a fluent answer. Try it!

Oral answers: debates and role play

A coursework assessment may contain a role play section. This may ask for you to play the part of a character involved in some sort of geographical decision. For example, you might be asked to pretend that you are a local councillor in a debate on a road widening scheme which is being proposed for a village high street. Preparation is vitally important if you are going to get as much out of the debate as you can (and therefore more marks).

In the example given, do you know what a local councillor does? This information is vital if you are going to speak up as your teacher hopes. Therefore, ask your teacher for the information. If you are told that it is all part of the exercise for you to find out, then ask around. Your school librarian might help. You could, of course, ring the local council to get the information 'straight from the horse's mouth'. If you do so, do not forget to put a note to that effect in your write-up of the debate. Teachers love initiative and they take it as a personal triumph if they have stimulated you to take such a step! Give them the excuse to give you more marks!

Written notes in preparation for an oral exercise are vital. The Prime Minister at Question Time in the House of Commons does not come up with answers 'off the cuff' very often. Usually, background information is provided by researchers which allows an informative, not to say correct, answer. You cannot be expected to be knowledgeable about a topic, particularly about the way a certain person might view it, without suitable preparation and notes. Hints on improving your ability in discussion are given in Section Three.

The grading system

At the end of the GCSE course, you will be given a grade on a seven-point scale. In England, Wales and Northern Ireland, that scale will be called grades A, B, C, D, E, F and G. In Scotland, the numbers 1 to 7 are used with awards being made at three levels, which are *Foundation Level* for grades 6 and 7, *General Level* for grades 3, 4 and 5 and *Credit Level* for grades 1 and 2. Each grade measures your **positive achievement** and tells a future employer what you know, understand and can do in the subject. As an example, Table 2.3 shows what is expected of candidates being awarded grades F and C. You will notice that F does *not* say that the candidate cannot do a number of things. It stresses what that candidate **has achieved**.

The grades will be awarded following the completion of the course. They will recognize what the candidate has achieved both in **coursework assessments** and in the **examination**. Unlike in the traditional

Ability	Grade F	Grade C
	For grade F, the student is likely to have shown the ability to	For grade C, the student is likely to have shown the ability to
In relation to knowledge	Recall basic information	Recall a wide range of information
In relation to understanding and values	1 Have a simple understanding of the processes that give rise to both physical and human landscapes 2 Understand how one factor relates to another in explaining the environment 3 Show a simple understanding that people's values influence geographical decisions	1 Have a good understanding of the processes that give rise to both physical and human landscapes 2 Understand how these influence patterns of settlement, land use etc. 3 Understand how these patterns change over time 4 Describe and account for the way factors influence one another in explaining the environment 5 Be able to understand models of environmental systems 6 Show a good understanding of people's values and perceptions and how they influence geographical decisions
In relation to skills	1 Observe and record geographical data 2 Use a variety of different sources including maps 3 Draw simple sketch maps and diagrams (e.g. bar graphs) 4 Communicate information by brief statements 5 Suggest possible solutions to geographical issues	1 Select relevant data from a variety of sources 2 Interpret and present information in various forms 3 Use geographical concepts and principles to interpret geographical situations 4 Suggest possible consequences of certain processes 5 Propose and justify possible solutions to geographical issues

Table 2.3 Grade descriptions

examination system where separate marks were given each time a correct fact was repeated in answer to the question asked, candidates will be expected to reach a certain **standard** of answer to achieve a certain mark. These marks will then be put together to suggest the grade that candidate has achieved. Answers will not be point marked, but will be compared against the knowledge, understanding and skills expected of candidates at each level of achievement. Candidates' mistakes will not be penalized. It is only **positive achievement** which will be considered.

Marking will take place during the course. This will be done by your teacher, probably working together with other teachers from nearby schools.

At some point in the course, the standards set by one school will be checked against those of others to ensure that you are not being marked harder or softer than anyone else. A representative of the Examination Group will in addition take a sample of all the coursework at the end of the two years to check the accuracy of the marking. Finally, the examination at the end of the course will be marked by an external examiner (not your teacher). This means that standards can be compared between schools. All the evidence will be put together at the end to give a grade for each candidate.

Checklist 3 Approaching coursework questions

1 Plan your answer carefully. You could write a list of key words in order to produce a 'flowing' answer.

2 Make sure you have the right information to allow you to answer the question properly.

3 Write enough to enable you to get a good grade.

Planning your own enquiry

Some time during your GCSE geography course, you will be asked to complete some fieldwork. This may be designed for you, as it would be in a **Teacher-Planned Enquiry**, or it may just be asked for as part of an **Individual Study** or personal enquiry. In this case, you will need to decide what type of fieldwork is required, plan it yourself, arrange the equipment you will need and carry it out. Fieldwork is used in GCSE as a base for learning, not as an end in itself. It should not be purely descriptive but should analyse, evaluate and point out the general importance of the study.

Physical studies are only in the spirit of GCSE if they look at the people-environment relations. For example, the way in which flooding affects settlements is a GCSE style study, but measuring river flow by itself is not. This section is concerned with planning your work.

Choosing a title

If you are asked to produce an Individual Study or a fieldwork report, a good way to start is to ask yourself which section of the syllabus interests you most. If this lends itself to fieldwork, you are on your way. For instance, you might enjoy studying the internal structure of towns. You could easily investigate this topic in the field. On the other hand, if you enjoy studying the Third World, it will be highly unlikely that you will be able to carry out any fieldwork in that respect and you must therefore look at another area.

Once you have selected an area in which you are interested, you must think of a topic you could study. One way you could get ideas about suitable areas of study would be to look through the index of a geography text book. Possible areas could be found by referring to the correct section in the text. Your eventual title **must** be a question. In this way your study will fit the pattern that the examiner is expecting. The next consideration is whether the title you are suggesting is one that you can actually answer. Here are some points to consider:

1 Have you got access to the information you will need in order to answer the question? For instance, if you ask, 'Why did Smith and Co move to Leeds?' you must be able to talk with someone involved in the decision. If the company is large enough to have its own records department, can you get permission to use it or to interview somebody there? You can even arrive at your question the other way round. If you have a lot of information available on a particular topic, you could work out a question which could be answered, at least in part, from that information.

2 Is the question manageable? For example, if you ask, 'What is the pattern of commuting from Southampton?' you are posing an enormous question. You might find some published figures, but unless you carry out your own fieldwork, you may not be able to obtain all the marks available. A better question, and one you could manage yourself, might be, 'What is the pattern of journeys to work from Sholing (a suburb of Southampton)?' You would not be expected to ask everyone from Sholing where they work and how they travel there. Your fieldwork could include traffic counts and sample surveys to suggest what the pattern might be.

3 Is the question too easy to answer? 'Is the land next to the River Thames likely to flood?' can be answered simply. The answer is yes! The question would be better rephrased. 'How has the likelihood of flooding of the Thames near Maidenhead affected the management of the land?' might be one possible question. 'Does flooding of the Thames influence transport in the Maidenhead area?' not only allows you to investigate transport routes, but also allows the inclusion of traffic counts and the investigation of old newspaper reports.

4 Is the question too dangerous to answer? 'What is the sphere of influence of 'The Traveller's Arms?' might be an easily managed study, with plenty of fieldwork techniques that could be used, but if it involves interviewing people as they leave the premises, perhaps you had better think again! Equally, 'What are the temperature changes up a steep scarp slope near Birdlip?' might put you at risk if you are involved in measuring temperatures on steep rocky slopes. This question also illustrates another possible pitfall:

5 Is the question in the spirit of the GCSE? This particularly applies to physical studies. Most examination groups do not allow solely physical studies. The above question must therefore be carefully phrased to include a human element. Thus, 'Does microclimate affect farming in the Birdlip area?' would be a far better title. This would allow not only the measurement of temperature changes, wind patterns and shade but also of land use. It also allows you to interview farmers.

6 Do you have the right equipment to allow you to answer the question? 'How is the noise from aircraft taking off affected by weather conditions?' may be a very stimulating study, but if you cannot accurately measure the noise, preferably with a decibel counter, your study will be doomed. You could involve people by asking, 'How is Winkfield affected by Heathrow airport?' This would allow a small section on aircraft noise, perhaps measured by people's reactions rather than direct measurement, but it would also allow studies of where people work and whether they use the airport for holidays.

The planning sheet (Fig. 2.6) shows how you can use all these points to enable you to decide on a title.

Breaking down your question

Once you have decided on your overall question, you should divide it into subsections. Each of these can allow you to demonstrate your skill in a different area of the subject or in a different technique. The easiest way to explain this point is to give an example:

Overall question:
What is the pattern of use of Woolworth's, Welshpool?

Sub-question 1: How many people use the store . . .

Fig. 2.6. A SAMPLE FIELDWORK/INDIVIDUAL STUDY PLANNING SHEET

1. Name. *David Lowe 4 S*

2. General Area of Interest *Farming*

_____

3. Topics which might be looked at through fieldwork *Land use related to soil, distance, slope, drainage etc. Changes over time. Crop yield and climate.*

4. Possible question *What factors affect the choice of land use on Home Farm ?*

Checklist:- 1. Data available?   Y/N
2. Manageable size?   Y/N
3. Enough in the question?   Y/N
4. Safety?   Y/N
5. Physical/human elements contained? Y/N
6. Equipment available?   Y/N
7. Permission obtained (if necessary)   Y/N *From Mr Green*

If Y to the first 6, and 7 if necessary, go on........
5. Breaking down the question. Sub-questions....
a) *What is the land use in 1989?*
b) *How are the following arranged on the farm? — soil depth, rock type, pH values, drainage, slope, microclimate.*
c) *What is the farmer's management plan? (use of animals, fertilizers, pesticides, rotation etc).*
d) *What socio - economic factors affect the farm (markets, work force, subsidies, age of farmer etc) ?*

CHECK YOUR PROGRESS AT THIS POINT WITH YOUR TEACHER. *J.S. Jones* (sig)

6. Equipment needed. _____

MAPS — 1:25,000 of farm. Geology map.

Indentification book of crops.

Soil pH meter, clinometer, weather instruments (whirling hygrometer, anemometer).

Questionnaire

7. Equipment availability (dates) *August 18th to 22nd*

Collect from: *Peter Robinson, 2 Swallow Way (664312)*

Return to: *Sally James, 5, Clower Ave. (552136)*

8. Pilot study? *Phone call to Mr. Green to check appointment to answer questionnaire and permission for w.b. August 18th*

_____

9. Fieldwork dates: *August 18th to 22nd*

_____

10. CHECKED BY *J.S. Jones* _____ (TEACHER)

Janice Lowe _____ (PARENT)

Fig. 2.6 A sample fieldwork/individual study planning sheet

a) throughout a typical day? (To be found by carrying out a pedestrian count on a sample basis)

b) throughout the week? (To be found by interviewing the store manager)

c) throughout the year? (To be found by interview, plus Tourist Board figures)

Sub-question 2: A **sphere of influence** is the area within which shoppers look to that store for supplies of various types. What is the store's sphere of influence? (To be found by interviewing shoppers)

Sub-question 3: How do people use the shop? (For which items, how frequently? How do they travel to the store?) These could again be found from a shopping survey.

Planning your strategy

‘Organization and planning are vital to any sort of personal investigation work.’

Having broken your question into its constituent parts, you can use them to plan out the equipment you will need, the timing of your fieldwork, the contacts you will have to make and the background research you will have to carry out. This is shown on the sample planning sheet (Fig. 2.6). Make sure that you check the feasibility of the work you are suggesting with an adult, preferably a teacher or a parent, before you finalize your overall plan. The **safety rules** (see page 23) are very important at this point.

A pilot study?

One way of seeing whether something will work or not is to carry out a pilot study. This could take the form of asking a few people the questions on your questionnaire to see whether you are getting the right answers. A pilot study could be made by taking a few measurements to see whether the equipment chosen and the method selected are workable. Whatever the example, the idea of a pilot study is to achieve an efficient method of collecting data. The method allows you to iron out any inconsistencies and problems before going on to the main part of the study.

Fieldwork

Actual methods of fieldwork are discussed in Section Four. The planning of the work should take into account how far you have to travel, the weather conditions you are likely to meet and who should be informed about where and when you are working. Above all, it should take into consideration **safety factors**. These are just as important as the data collection methods, which should obviously also be carefully planned. The planning sheet (Fig. 2.6) can again be used for satisfying yourself that you have done everything necessary before going out into the field.

Analysis and the write up

When you have all your data, you should use a diary planner (e.g. Fig. 2.1) to ensure that you keep to the deadline required. Before you begin the write-up it is most important that you refer once again to your teacher. Do not forget that, even at this stage, you still have the figures to illustrate and analyse, a report to write and conclusions to make. **Never** throw away your field or rough notes. Certain examining groups expect them to be handed in with coursework. The final report should contain the following sections:

Extract

This should be about a hundred words and act as a quick reference for the examiner (your teacher). It should say what the study is about, indicate the main finding and say whether there were any problems in setting it up. The best time to write this is after you have written the main report.

Introduction

This sets the scene, poses the question and indicates why you chose the area you did. It contains a statement of the **aims** of the study.

Methods used

Each separate investigation should have a description of the methods you used. It should refer to any sampling you did, any modifications you made as you went along and any problems you faced (together with how you overcame them). This section can be planned early on but added to once you have finished the work.

Results obtained

These should be shown in tables, maps, diagrams and writing and should be clearly labelled and titled. They should be referred to easily in the text. This is the first part of the survey to be written up.

Analysis

This should indicate the main trends you found in the data. Also show how these influence the question you posed. Outline any predictions you can make from the data you have gathered or explanations you can offer. Finally, give the answer to the original question. This is where you use your skills of interpretation. It is the section which will be looked at very closely by the examiners to sort out the better candidates. You might be tempted to ask further questions having got this far, or you may be able to come to:

Conclusions

These might link your study to broader geographical models (or generalizations). For instance, if you are studying the layout of a town such as Matlock, you could conclude by saying how it relates to one of the models of urban structure (concentric, sector or multiple nuclei). You might even be able to suggest a model of your own! This is the section in which you can also mention attitudes, values and judgements.

Others

In addition, you should have a table of **contents** at the start of the study (like at the start of this book), a **bibliography**, containing a list of all the sources you used, and any **appendix** items you might wish to include (at the end), such as base maps, questionnaires or pamphlets. The bibliography should list your sources in the following order:

**Name of book, author, publisher, date,
e.g. 'Revise Geography', Bolwell and Lines, Charles Letts, 1987**

Safety rules

These are **most** important and should be treated seriously.

1 Always inform adults about your fieldwork. Let them know where you will be and when. Take some identification with you.

2 Always work in twos or threes if possible.

3 Always wear the right clothing for the job. For example, light coloured or reflective clothing is best if you are conducting a traffic survey.

4 Never take unnecessary risks either with studies in the countryside (steep slopes, rivers, woodlands etc.) or in urban areas ('strangers', traffic etc.).

5 Always take a good map with you and have an idea of what to do if anything goes wrong!

The importance of following strict safety rules cannot be stressed too greatly.

✓ Checklist 4 Planning your own enquiry

1 Choose your title very carefully.

2 Make sure you have, or can get, the information to enable you to answer the question.

3 Choose a question small enough to handle but large enough to be important.

4 Don't choose a question with an obvious answer.

5 Don't choose a question with a very complex answer.

6 Always be aware of the **safety rules**.

7 Make sure that any physical question has enough on the human or environment side to make it a GCSE question.

8 Make sure that you have the right equipment for the job.

9 Use a planning sheet to make sure that your work is efficient.

10 Break down your question into its constituent parts.

11 Consider conducting a pilot survey.

12 Use a variety of techniques in your fieldwork.

13 Plan your writing up to include all the elements asked for in your syllabus.

14 Present your enquiry well, with contents, chapters, appendix and bibliography, all presented in a folder or binder.

Hints on improving your skills and techniques

The skills you will need to use during your GCSE course can count for nearly half of the total marks. The contribution of skills to coursework is shown in Appendix 1. They are also needed in many ways in the final examination. The skills and techniques dealt with in this section are those shown in Table 1.1. Skills and techniques of investigation however (especially data collection techniques), are dealt with in Section Four.

Communication skills

Speaking up: debates and discussions

At various times throughout the course, you will be expected to contribute verbally in some way. You may be asked simply to answer questions in class. It is also likely that you will be asked to take part in discussions, debates and role play exercises. The very thought of speaking out loud to the rest of your class may horrify you. Since you will have to do it, however, it is much better to be prepared and overcome any fears you may have. You should always be prepared to **ask** sensible questions and to take the **initiative** in discussions. There are various techniques you can use to improve your performance in verbal communication.

The importance of **planning** in oral work has already been mentioned above (page 17). This section is particularly concerned with ways in which you can **practise** to improve your performance. To begin with, you will never improve at anything unless you practise. Some people are content to say 'I'm too shy,' or 'I wish I could speak up like that!' The fact is, however, that being able to speak in public is an **acquired** skill, not an inherited one! How can you help yourself to acquire the skill?

The ability to speak up well can be learnt.

Firstly, it is no good to think what you might say in your mind without actually trying it. If you are asked to prepare your contribution to a debate, don't just plan it out. Actually speak it to someone or even something! The 'something' could be an imaginary listener in the safety of your bedroom, or it could be a tape recorder so that you can play your performance back and listen to your efforts. There might be a willing brother or sister around to help, but it would probably be better if a group of you from your class got together to practise your contributions. Whichever way you practise, you will need some organization first.

Next, you must be prepared to **listen**. If you are really discussing, rather than adding to a list of loosely related facts, you will respond to points that have already been made. In the heat of a debate, it may be difficult to remember what somebody else has said. The next thing you must do, therefore, is to **make good notes**. You will probably be asked to write about the debate in some way at the end, so your notes should help you to remember. The main thing is to be **consistent** in your note making. Here is an example.

In a classroom debate about whether a new power station should be built at Fawley on Southampton Water, one contributor, Hazel, playing the part of a CEGB representative, said:

> I am very much in favour of the power station being built there for the following very good reasons. Firstly, there is already a large oil-fired power station next to the proposed site. This means that the area has

an existing trained work force and supply routes, both to and from the power station. Next, the site is near an area of large demand, with all the industry and areas of population growth along Southampton Water and the coastal plain towards Portsmouth. In addition, any environmental pollution and visual damage caused by power production is best concentrated in one area rather than being spread more widely.

If you tried to write down everything that Hazel said, you would not be able to take part in the debate. You would be writing all the time! Instead, take a look at the notes that Colin took from Hazel's contribution:

CEGB rep. – FOR
1 Near existing station
2 Big local demand
3 Pollution concentration

In about ten words, Colin managed to note the more important points that Hazel was making. In particular, he noted that she supported the proposal and he listed her reasons. He did not attempt to write down the fine detail. Hopefully, what he wrote would remind him of that at a later stage.

Try making notes from a radio news broadcast in order to practise this art. It is not easy, and at first you will want to write down everything. If you can persuade an adult to help you, ask whether you can give a run down of the evening's news, using your notes to jog your memory. Hopefully, you will remember the details without even having written them down. If you can succeed with a news bulletin, you will certainly succeed with a classroom debate! You might like to use abbreviations in your notes, such as UK, CBD and Mt. You will probably recognize those. What about 'cons' however? It is not a standard abbreviation, so does it mean conservative, construction engineer, conservationist or one of many other possibilities? The way to overcome this problem is to write it out in full the first time you use it, together with your abbreviation. Every subsequent time you use it you can shorten it, e.g. Conservationist (Cons) – against. New sta. = much more pollution.

The main thing to realize about oral work in class is that what you have got to say is as important as what anyone else has to offer. Once you have persuaded yourself of this fact, you will become a noted speaker. It might as well be you as anyone else!

When you take part in a role play exercise, try to **act in role**. In the above example, the representative from the CEGB would deal in 'facts' given to her by the research department at the CEGB. If challenged, she would be likely to say that the facts have been established by widespread research and, if pushed further, that any additional information would have to be obtained from them to ensure that it was correct. She would probably not be drawn to make rash statements on matters which are so sensitive. She would probably offer to supply answers once she had checked them with her department. She would say that the supply of electricity is fundamental to modern life and counts above almost anything else if living standards are to be maintained.

The conservationist could also take this line, but on the whole would see things in a much simpler way. New industry would bring with it the threat of greater pollution. Conservationists generally see themselves as guardians of the environment, on both a local and global scale. Complicated financial or industrial arguments can cut little ice with them. They usually try to distil the argument to one of the quality of life.

Of course, what has just been said could lead to the argument that the participants in the debate have been 'stereotyped'. This means that the descriptions are of a common image of the CEGB representative and the conservationist rather than of real people. We must be careful that we don't go too far along this track. For example, despite what a lot of people thought at first, Bob Geldof showed himself to be much more of an organizer, humanitarian and public speaker than any of them would have

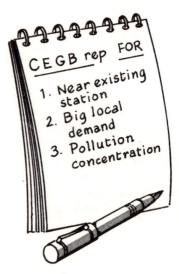

Fig. 3.1 Notes from a debate

Practise writing very brief notes which will say enough to jog your memory.

given him credit for just by looking at him. He did not fit his 'stereotype'. Appearances and the jobs people do are not always good predictors of how they will react, but in a GCSE role play exercise you will find it easier if you play the part as expected. Unless you are given a little description of your character first, you should write one for yourself before you begin. You will then find it easier to act in role.

Example

You are asked to play the part of a shopkeeper in Fawley, near to where the new power station would be built. Here are two possible characters and the way they might then react:

Fig. 3.2 Shopkeeper 1

Shopkeeper 1   Male, 32 years old, keen on sport, ambitious to own a larger store, married, two children under the age of six.

Reaction: *for*. Building workers would spend in his shop. More people for his local football team. Can buy a larger store or move out of area once he has made the profits, since he has no ties to secondary schools yet.

Fig. 3.3 Shopkeeper 2

Shopkeeper 2   Female, 57 years old, lived in the area all her life, loves gardening, not married.

Reaction: *against*. Regrets change in a beautiful area on the fringes of The

New Forest. Pollution threat to plants. Does not want to leave because all her friends are in Fawley and would be lonely if she moved elsewhere.

Whichever character you choose, try to react as that person would and **be consistent** with the points you make.

If you are not very confident before a class discussion of any kind, you could get together with a group of friends to discuss your particular part. Sometimes you can help yourself and your group by making a display (a poster or collection of items) about what you will be discussing. You may be asked to do this by your teacher, but it helps you to sort out your ideas anyway.

Improving your written work

There are a few basic rules to follow if you are going to improve your written communication and they are very simple. You may have already acquired the skills by the time you are studying for your GCSE, but it is never too late to be reminded of them! Remember that nothing comes easily, however. If you are going to take advantage of these tips, you will have to practise them. Apply these ideas to the next piece of written work you hand in and judge your next move based on your teacher's reaction.

Rule one

Neat layout can make even untidy writing look good.

Write as clearly as you can. Take a bit of trouble to dot your i's and cross your t's. The easiest way to ensure this is to leave time before you hand in your work to *check* it thoroughly. *Space* your work out so that different sections are clearly separated. Start a *new paragraph* every time you come to a new idea or example. Like this, there will also be room to make any alterations or additions at a later time. Make sure before you begin a piece of work that you have the right *implements* to finish the job. There is nothing more infuriating than struggling to read writing done with a dying biro, or coming across a complete change of colour halfway through a piece of work. Remember, typing or wordprocessing *is* allowed.

Rule two

Use headings, titles and numbers wherever appropriate. Your examiner (teacher) will want to be able to find the question number you are answering as easily as possible. All maps and diagrams *must* have a title. In a piece of work like an individual study or a fieldwork report, a figure number is also a good idea. A good rule to follow is that if you think you need a diagram to illustrate something, the title could easily be the next line of text. For example, if you were writing about the site of a village and you said that it was originally a dry point site, your diagram could show what a dry point site is. The title could therefore be . . .

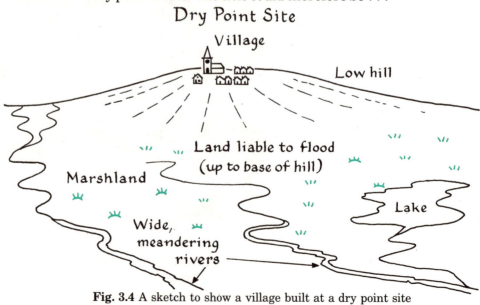

Fig. 3.4 A sketch to show a village built at a dry point site

Be sure to refer to the diagram in your writing, but do not give a lengthy description of what it shows. You will only be given the marks once.

Rule three

Plan your work before you write. This is very important if you are going to be writing a lot. It is easy to go off at a tangent, ending up by not answering the question set.

Example

You are asked to explain why large stores tend to group together in the centre of towns. This could be your plan:

Need large pop. – e.g. – threshold – centre of market area – sphere – accessible – service area – range of a good – shared infrastructure – competition and comparison.

A small amount of time taken in writing a brief plan can lead to a much more logical answer.

Translated into a written answer, this plan leads to the following:

Large stores, departmental and chain stores, often group together in the centres of towns. For example, in the same street in the centre of Reading are Boots, W.H. Smith, Dolcis, Millwards, Curry's (chain stores) and Heelas, Debenhams, Marks and Spencer and BHS (department stores) amongst others. This is because they all need a lot of people within easy reach of them.

The number of people required before a particular enterprise can exist is called its threshold population. For large stores this threshold is large. For Marks and Spencer stores, it is 20 000. The population occurs in an area which is called the sphere of influence. The stores are usually as central as possible to this area so that they are as accessible as possible to their potential customers. Since roads lead in to the centre of settlements, the stores tend to cluster where these roads join, in the centre itself.

Stores are also able to service this area efficiently, whether it be by sending out deliveries or by supplying service engineers to deal with problems with equipment that has been purchased from them. The delivery area, known as the range of a good, is determined by the distance an item can be sent out from the service centre before the transport becomes so costly that it would be cheaper for a customer to buy elsewhere. The best place to locate is in the centre of a large market area for this reason. In addition, stores at a town centre location benefit from shared services. The same car parks can be used by all the customers for town centre stores. They use the same infrastructure (roads, electricity supply, gas, telephone service etc.). They all thrive on competition and comparison. People will travel a long way if they are going to be able to 'shop around' for either cheaper items or better quality items. They can do this if stores are close together.

Try to write some practice plans for yourself.

Example

Set yourself the target of writing a list of no more than 25 words each time to enable you to answer the following questions.

a) Describe how land use varies away from a town. (4)

b) Explain why market gardening tends to occur near a town, but animal rearing tends to be further away. (4)

c) How can average income be used to measure the development of a country? (5)

d) Imagine you are a government official. Your government has decided to expand its nuclear electricity generation programme. Explain to a meeting of villagers, near whose village a new nuclear power station will be built, why you think it is in the country's interest to build a nuclear power station. (6)

Once you have written these practice plans, you can take the next step and translate them into actual written answers. You will find that you get faster at this as you practise and you should find that your answers improve if you use the system well.

If you follow these simple rules, your written communication should improve in clarity, accuracy and style, any of which could lead to an improvement in marks.

Improving your drawing

A frequently heard cry from students is that they are not artistic and cannot draw neat maps and diagrams. The two are not the same, however. You might not be artistic, but there is no excuse for not drawing neatly. There is a lot you can do to improve your standard of presentation, if nothing else. The actual techniques of presenting information are dealt with in Section Four, but here are some ways in which you can improve your performance in this area. Hints 1 and 2 apply to all your work. Hint 3 is particularly for the examination, but will help you to draw relevant maps in coursework as well.

Hint 1

The correct equipment and a bit of practice can make up for any lack of artistic ability.

Always use the correct equipment. Do not try to draw a thin, accurate line with an HB pencil! You will need that for sketching, but you should use a hard lead pencil for accurate graph and diagram work. A list of the equipment you need as a geography student is given in Section Two (Planning Your Work).

Hint 2

Practise drawing sketches and diagrams to illustrate any complex ideas which are difficult to express in words. For example, if you are trying to explain why coastal protection measures are so difficult in the area around Christchurch Bay in Hampshire and Dorset, a cross section of the cliffs can be used and annotated (notes added) to explain the situation far quicker and more clearly than is possible in words. Figure 3.5 shows how this can be achieved. You can use the method given as Hint 3 to remember such diagrams for examinations. Diagrams should be used wherever they provide a short cut to understanding. They should not repeat something you have already said in writing and they should not need a lot of extra explanation to go with them. They are 'geographical shorthand' and should be quick, clear and explicit ways of showing relationships.

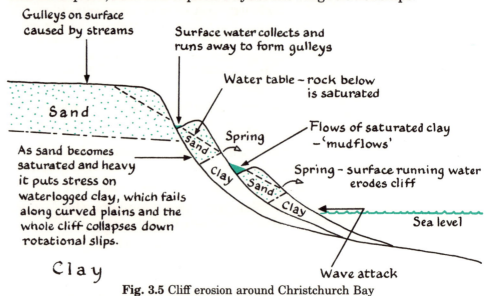

Fig. 3.5 Cliff erosion around Christchurch Bay

Hint 3

Learn a selection of useful sketch maps for examinations. In most syllabuses, you can illustrate work on topics, for example industrial decline, with case studies you have learnt yourself. For instance, you may have learnt about industrial decline in North East England. You cannot possibly remember all the details of settlements, industries, rivers, coastline, communications etc., so you must first decide what it is that you can show usefully on a map to illustrate this topic. The main points you need to show are that in the past industries were based on coal mining, iron and steel and shipbuilding, the so-called 'traditional' industries. Secondly, the North East of England is a long way from markets and suppliers. It is what is usually called a 'peripheral' area. These two facts are the main geographical points you can illustrate on the map. There are obviously other historical points such as government policy, world industrial changes in both materials and competitors and changes in world trade which also help to explain the decline, but these do not lend themselves to being shown on a map. A map drawn using the information above would look like Fig. 3.6. Note that it has a border and a key, some idea of a scale and a north pointer.

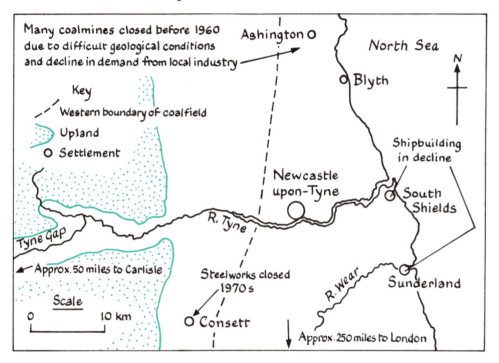

If you are drawing a sketch map in examination conditions, you will not be able to give a scale, so approximate distances are useful.

Fig. 3.6 Industrial decline in North East England

Having achieved a base map with which you are happy, you should set about learning it. Do not try to do it all at once. If you take it in stages, you will be able to remember it remarkably quickly. Start by drawing the basic shape of the coast and main rivers. In this example, you have three lines to draw inside the border. On a blank piece of paper, draw the border shape and then the three lines to represent the rivers and the coast. Check what you have drawn with the original. Keep drawing the basic map over and over until you can remember the shape. This is a particularly easy example, but you will be surprised how you can conquer quite complicated shapes this way. Having learnt your basic map, you can now add the details shown in Fig. 3.6. Repeat the process of sketching, referring to the original and checking. When you are confident that you have learnt it, put it to one side and remember to test yourself the next day. You will need to keep a record of the examples you have learnt so that you can test yourself on all of them nearer to the examination.

 Checklist 5 Improving skills and techniques

Communication skills
1 Verbal:
  a) Plan your work by writing notes.

  b) Practise what you are going to say.

c) Listen in any discussion. Don't just try to make your own points. Listen to other people as well.

d) Make good notes during discussions.

e) Act in role in role play exercises.

2 Written:

a) Write as clearly as you can.

b) Space out your work.

c) Always have the right tools for the job.

d) Always plan your written work carefully.

e) Use headings, titles and numbers wherever appropriate.

f) Always refer to diagrams, maps, photographs etc. in your writing if you have included them.

3 Drawing:

a) Always use the right equipment.

b) Practice makes perfect! Don't expect to be 'artistic' without trying!

c) Learn maps and diagrams by drawing them frequently.

Interpretation skills

Improving your reasoning

It is a real art to be able to put what you understand about a topic into words. It is even more of an art to be able to talk about it. You might be asked to talk about something you have been studying, for example a map or a photograph, or you might be called upon to respond in a debate to what somebody else is saying.

The method of writing and interpreting notes shown in Figs. 3.7 and 3.8 is as good for written work as it is for oral work. You can practise the method by using it with passages taken from geography text books. Later, you can apply it in debates or role play exercises in class. Since you will have to develop a good speed with this technique by the time you apply it to oral work, it is best to practise from written work first.

Often the first stage in preparing for what you are going to say is to write something down. The way you should approach note making is described in point 1 below and shown in Fig. 3.7. Making notes from what somebody

Text: It is difficult to define what we mean by 'Developing' countries. One item which sets them apart is the fact that most people work in Primary industries, many of them as farmers and most of those as subsistence farmers. Consequently, incomes and the intake of calories per head are also low. It is difficult for children to be sent to school, if one exists in the local area, because they are needed to help work the land, especially at harvest time. The illiteracy rate is often high in Developing countries as a result. All these points tend to give a negative image of Developing countries, but it is also true that some diseases such as cancer and heart disease have a much lower incidence in these countries. There are also very strong family ties. Families work together and look after their children and elders as a unit. In some ways, therefore, they could teach the 'Developed world' a lot.

Notes

Developing – most work in Primary – subsistence farmers
Low incomes and intake of calories } Negative
Children help with the work on the land – illiteracy rate high
Positive – some diseases less common and families work together

Fig. 3.7 Making notes from written information

else has just said is explained in the section on verbal communication skills on page 25.

1 If you are commenting on some written information, you need to produce some brief notes about it to use as a 'crib sheet' as you are talking. If you are working from your own notes, you could go through and highlight the most important words in your notes. Be careful as you do this because you will be tempted to underline everything. An example is given in Fig. 3.7. Obviously, if you are working from a book or other printed information, you will not be able to underline or highlight in the same way. Your next step is to transfer the words you have picked out or underlined on to another sheet of paper to remind you of what the notes were saying. (In a way, this is the reverse of the method suggested above for writing an essay plan.) You should then use this list to pick out the information which needs further explanation, or information upon which you need to comment.

2 You can now plan to make your response more logical. You can first further highlight points to which you need to reply. Then you can make a plan for what you need to say. An example is given in Fig. 3.8. You might think that this process takes a long time, but with a little practice it can easily be adapted for use in debates or class discussions.

Fig. 3.8 Interpreting the notes

Most work in Primary – Primary industries = farming, fishing, forestry, mining. As countries become more Developed, lower percentages work on land because farming is more efficient and more jobs are available in manufacturing and the services. Most farmers have a very small area of land, but need to farm intensively.

Low incomes – subsistence farming often gives no income at all. Trade in the market can be by exchange (barter). Some farmers become trapped in a vicious cycle, ending up by having to give part of their harvest to the landlord (sharecropping). Diets are often poor as a result (intake of calories).

Illiteracy rate high – this can be a problem for spreading information about new farming techniques and hygiene. It can also hold back industrialization

Positive points – the family spirit is often better in the Developing world, especially in the care of the elderly. Common diseases of the Developed world such as heart disease and liver complaints, both often brought on by over-eating and drinking, are very uncommon, although other illnesses can be rife and medical aid is often poor.

Sometimes you may be able to show how things relate to one another by making notes on a **star diagram**. This method can help you to picture how the individual parts fit together. The following star diagram (Fig. 3.9) shows the factors that affect the location of a factory.

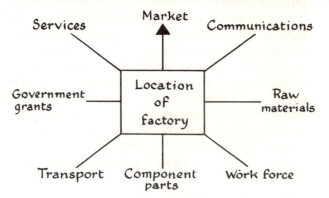

Fig. 3.9 A star diagram to show factors which influence the location of a factory

Another sort of diagram which allows you to see how things fit together is the **flowchart**. This is used, in particular, to show how one thing leads onto another (Fig. 3.10).

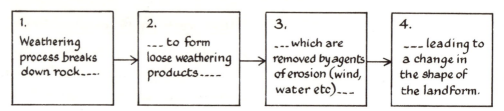

Fig. 3.10 Stages in landscape change

Interpretation skills

Interpreting written material

The method you can use for interpreting what another writer is saying is shown in the section above. This describes note making as the first step. The method is as good for working from a text as it is for working from your notes about what somebody else is saying. Figure 3.8 shows how you can approach the interpretation of the notes you have made in the first place.

Interpreting photographs

Photographs are used in nearly all GCSE examination papers. In addition, you might want to use them to illustrate your own fieldwork or Individual Study. If you include them, you should always write some comment on photographs, since they are not just meant to be pretty. They should add to your discussion of a point. You can use the techniques outlined below so that you can get as much out of the photographs as possible.

Traditionally, photographs in books and examinations have been in black and white. There has been a recent move to print them in colour, however, which helps you to pick out important points more easily. In the present instance, black and white photographs will be used. If you can interpret *them*, you will find the colour versions even easier!

The first example given (Fig. 3.11) is of a rural scene in the West Indies. Examples of typical questions which demand some kind of interpretation of the photograph are given below.

Question 1

Name one possible cause for the soil erosion shown in the photograph.   (2)

Interpretation You must remember that you were told the location of the photograph in the introduction to the question. Although wind can be

Fig. 3.11 A rural scene in the West Indies

a major cause of soil erosion, it is unlikely to be the main reason in the West Indies given the humid climate.

Use clues in the photograph to link your answer to the location. The slopes are steep. There are some animals (goats) grazing on this slope. Putting the two together, the animals have probably removed the vegetation, leaving at least some of the soil exposed during periods of heavy rain. In fact, this area of the West Indies has a wet and a dry season as well, which adds to the problem, but you could not know that from the photograph.

Never read too much into the picture. For instance, you might just have been lucky enough to go to this island on holiday, or even have relatives there! You may happen to know that one reason for soil erosion there is that the view from this spot is a spectacular one and that hundreds of people per week walk over this area, thus causing erosion. The problem with this information is that there is no evidence for it on the photograph. It is better, therefore, to choose one of the safe options for which there is evidence, such as overgrazing. Your full answer thus might be:

Answer 1

Overgrazing by animals might lead to exposure of bare soil and erosion by rain water.

Note that the word 'might' is used since you are asked to name a possible cause.

Question 2

What measures could be taken to overcome the problems shown in the photograph? (4)

With photographs or maps, only say what you can see, even if you know the area well. You must have evidence for what you say.

Interpretation Once again, make your answer relevant. You could talk about how to stop gulleying, how to prevent wind erosion or even how to control trampling by sightseers. None of these things would be relevant to the location in the photograph, however. You could use sketches of the slope in the photograph to enable you to highlight the relation between your answer and the question. An example of this is shown in Fig. 3.12. The diagram shows firstly the hillside as it is and secondly a number of measures relevant to both this slope and the West Indies that could be taken to solve the problem. The diagram could be used almost by itself in answer to the question, depending on how detailed your notes are to go with it. You might like to add to your answer some examples from relevant areas of the world which show where successful schemes have been put into operation.

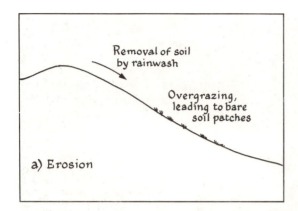
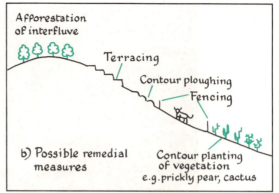

a) Erosion

b) Possible remedial measures

Fig. 3.12 Erosion of a slope in the West Indies and possible remedial measures

Answer 2

Figure 3.12 should first be reproduced.

Some examples of possible solutions to the soil erosion problem are shown in Fig. 3.12. Terracing has been successfully used in Colombia, South America, where the steep slopes of the Andes suffer badly from soil erosion brought on by the local farming practices. Terraces are formed by low walls built around the contours, with land flattened behind them. Contour planting of vegetation barriers (planting of vegetation around the contours of the hill) is common in North Africa in the foothills of the Atlas Mountains, for example in western Tunisia. These barriers must consist of vegetation which animals will not eat. Contour ploughing is also possible if the erosion is brought about by ploughing up and down the slope, as for instance in north east Brazil, where large areas of at times steep land are now used for the production of sugar cane. Fencing is against local custom in many areas, but has been very successfully introduced to stop overgrazing in southern Israel. Re-vegetating the hill top (interfluve) is a very important means of stopping erosion in inland areas of the Philippines.

Note that all the areas used as examples are in the tropical or sub-tropical regions in order to relate to the sort of area shown in the photograph. Although the examples given are very broad, they are qualified by further description. Never just quote 'Brazil' as an example since you could mean anything from the tropical forest area to the near-desert of the north east.

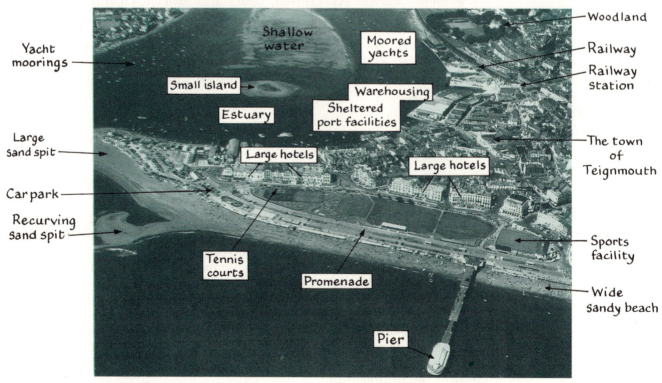

Fig. 3.13 Teignmouth.

Question 3

Name and locate one feature of marine deposition shown on the photograph of Teignmouth in Fig. 3.13. (2)

Interpretation You are usually given no indication of which direction the camera is pointing, so you should avoid compass points in your answer. It is quite acceptable to say 'top right', 'left foreground' and 'in the centre', but of course you should avoid using these terms if you also have an OS map with the photograph. You simply require the name of a feature and a place where it is found. Do not go into a lengthy description. If you have an OS map as well, give a grid reference.

Answer 3

Marine deposition feature: spit in the left foreground.

Question 4

Explain how the feature you have named might have been formed. (6)

Interpretation The answer may include a single well-labelled diagram to explain the formation of the spit. You certainly need a written explanation to go with this answer, but the diagram will help considerably. The answer might be as follows:

Answer 4

A spit is a finger-like projection of material, in this case made of sand, joined to the coast at one end and reaching out into an inlet. It has grown through the addition of particles eroded from further along the coast, possibly from cliffs. Particles have been moved along the coast by longshore drift, which occurs where waves break at an angle, carrying material up the beach in line with the direction of approach. The material then rolls down the slope of the beach and is again moved up at an angle by the next wave. The result is that it moves along the shore, forming a beach. When the waves come to an inlet, the beach builds out across it, forming a spit. Its growth is limited to the shallow water and it may curve inland due to tidal currents. It encloses sheltered water which often leads to silting and the growth of a salt marsh. (See Fig. 3.14)

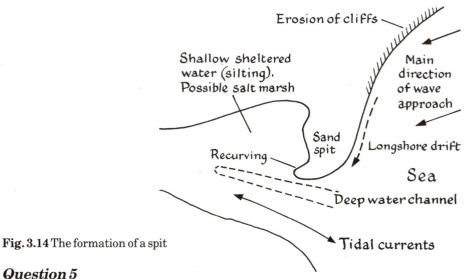

Fig. 3.14 The formation of a spit

Question 5

In what ways has the coast been used by people? (4)

Interpretation There are only four marks for this question, but a large number of things to mention. You might find that you keep saying things like, 'in the right foreground of the photograph, a pier can be seen, which indicates that the area is used for tourism'. This is rather long-winded and a better way might be to draw either a sketch or a sketch map to show the uses. You are not asked to explain the use, simply to say what it is.

Answer 5

An annotated sketch drawn from the photograph is shown in Fig. 3.15. This shows the uses of the coast.

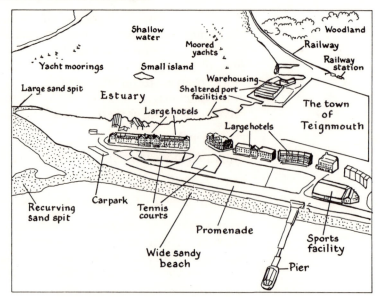

Fig. 3.15 The uses of the coast near Teignmouth

The way to improve your skills of analysing photographs is simply to practise techniques such as section drawing from photographs in text books or magazines. Since the problem with this is that you also have to write questions before you can answer them, here is a list of questions from the photograph of Teignmouth (Fig. 3.13). In all cases, you should use only the information on the photograph.

a) Explain why the harbour (left background) is well sited. (4)

b) Describe the street pattern of the town. (3)

c) Why might silting be a problem for the harbour? (3)

d) What things shown in the photograph might attract tourists to Teignmouth? (5)

e) There is a proposal to site a caravan park next to the woodland outside the built-up area (centre background). Explain why the residents of the town would have mixed reactions to the idea. (6)

Interpreting graphs and diagrams

The interpretation of data illustrated in graphs and diagrams is a very important skill you must master. During your GCSE course you will be given many examples of different graphs and diagrams to interpret and, certainly in the examination, they will play an important part. It is a very good idea to practise using them because of this. No matter what the question is that you are being asked, you must take a while to **look at** the graph or diagram, getting a general idea of what it shows. You can ask yourself the same basic questions every time in order to be able to answer any question put to you about the graph:

1 What does it show?

2 Why is it like that?

3 How will the figures illustrated affect other people or things?

The best way to show what this means is to use an example.

Example

Figure 3.16 shows the flow of traffic throughout the day on a road which leads to a city centre. Answering the three questions above for this graph:

1 Traffic volume is low (about 10 cars every 5 minutes) during the early morning until about 05.00 when it starts to increase rapidly. It reaches a peak of over 200 cars every 5 minutes just before 08.00 and is at a fairly steady rate of about 70 cars per 5 minutes for most of the morning. There

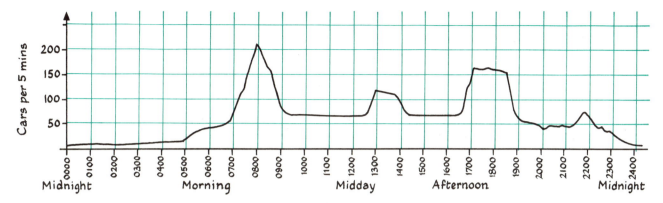

Fig. 3.16 Traffic on a suburban road through one day

is another peak of about 120 cars per 5 minutes between 12.30 and 14.00. The afternoon rate is about the same as during the morning. The early evening peak is about 170 cars per 5 minutes, but lasts for about 2 hours rather than the 1 in the morning. There is a decline to about 50 cars per hour for the rest of the evening until about 21.30, when there is another peak of about 80 cars per 5 minutes before the traffic again declines to a very low rate.

Summary: Low in early morning, 07.00 – 09.00 major increase, moderate traffic during rest of morning, mid-day peak, moderate afternoon traffic, 16.30 – 18.30 peak, lower early evening traffic, minor peak between 22.00 and 23.00

2 There is a morning 'rush' to work and school, business and shopping traffic during the morning, increased movement near midday due to travel at lunch time, business traffic during the afternoon, a more prolonged movement home in the evenings, therefore not reaching such a high peak, travel to entertainments during the evening and a mini rush home between about 22.00 and 23.00 in the evening.

3 There will probably be congestion in the morning and evening rush periods. People living near the road will suffer inconvenience, noise problems and possible pollution. Roads will need to be kept well surfaced to cope with traffic and junctions may have to be improved (roundabouts etc.).

You will be surprised how quickly you will be able to plan the answers to these basic questions in your mind after a little practice. The graph does not of course have to be a line graph. It could be a bar graph, a pie chart, a divided rectangle or one of a large number of other possible types. Figure 3.17 gives three more examples so that you can practise the technique. Two of the examples are graphs. The third is a diagram for which you can use exactly the same approach. Below are the actual questions asked in a piece of coursework assessment. Complete your answers to the basic questions as described above. Then plan out your answers to each question.

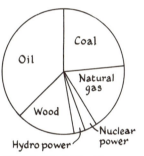

Fig. 3.17 a) World energy supplies, 1986

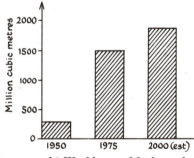

b) World use of fuel wood

c) The deforestation process

Questions

1 What proportion of the world's energy supplies came from **renewable** resources in 1986? (2)

2 Describe the changes in world demand for fuel wood over the period shown. (4)

3 How does Fig. 3.17(c) explain the fact that large areas of forest have been knocked down in Brazil between 1970 and the present? (5)

Using statistics

Sometimes you will be presented with a list or table of statistics and asked to write about them. It is easy to be confused by a large number of figures, so it is best to have a plan of attack when dealing with them. A look at the climate figures for one place will show what this means.

	J	F	M	A	M	J	J	A	S	O	N	D
Temperature °C	10	11	14	17	18	20	23	24	23	18	14	12
Precipitation mm	105	65	105	55	45	15	5	5	40	55	95	100

Table 3.1 Climate statistics for Lisbon

The first thing you should look at with any statistics is the high and low points. In the case of temperature for Lisbon (Table 3.1), it is hottest (maximum) in August and lowest (minimum) in January.

This **general pattern** is typical of all stations north of the equator.

Next, the **trend** should be looked at.

In the case of these temperatures, there is a steady rise from January to August and a steady fall thereafter.

There are no variations in this case, which is the third thing for which you should look. **Never** consider figures month by month. Look for patterns rather than separate facts. You should then look for some sort of overall figure relevant to the statistics being used.

Average yearly temperature would not mean much, since the figures are averages for each month already.

You could therefore give the highest and lowest figures and say that this is the range of temperatures for Lisbon.

This is more meaningful, since the further you get from the equator, the lower overall the temperatures become and the further inland you get for any given latitude, the more extreme they become (the larger the range becomes).

Summary

1 Maximum and minimum

2 Trend

3 Variations

4 Overall values (total, range)

Now apply this plan yourself to the precipitation figures for Lisbon.

This plan works not only for climate figures, but for such things as production and employment figures as well.

Look at the following statistics (Table 3.2) for the employment of workers at British Steel, Corby, from 1936 to 1986 and use the same plan to describe the main points about the statistics.

Year	Approx. number of workers	Year	Approx. number of workers
1936	2600	1966	13 500
1941	4800	1971	13 000
1946	6000	1976	13 000
1951	7000	1981	5000
1956	10 000	1986	0
1961	12 000		

Table 3.2 Workers at British Steel, Corby, 1936–86

You should be aware that statistics can hide variations at times. Look at a graph of the total number of workers employed at Corby (Fig. 3.18) and compare it with what you found by describing the statistics. The trends in the statistics look very steady, but the graph shows that some fluctuations occurred. They were hidden in the statistics because the figures were given for every five years and variations occurred between those dates.

One thing to take especial care with is the interval between values given in the statistics. The interval is the spacing between values, in this case the dates. Often the spacing can vary, giving a false impression unless you are aware of it. The population figures in Table 3.3 are of this sort. One way to interpret them more easily is to draw a graph of them first, making sure that the correct interval is given on the horizontal (x) axis.

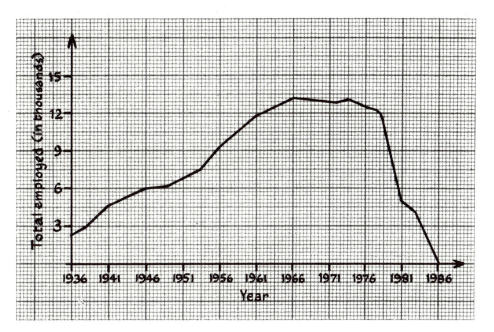

Fig. 3.18 Workers employed at British Steel, Corby 1936–86

Date	Total population (millions)
1750	800
1800	960
1850	1240
1900	1650
1930	2000
1950	2517
1960	2990
1970	3626
1980	4432
2000 (est)	6116

Table 3.3 World population totals, 1750–2000

> *Always make sure, when plotting any time series of data, that the horizontal axis has equal divisions.*

Practise using the plan given above to pick out the main elements in lists of statistics. You can also use it to highlight the differences and similarities between two sets of statistics, something you might well meet in analysing the results of your fieldwork or in examination questions.

How sketches can simplify an answer

Diagrams can be used as a sort of 'geographical shorthand' in order to explain complex matters which would otherwise take a lot of written explanation. It is very important that you practise the skills and techniques mentioned below since they can save you a great deal of time and clarify your ideas considerably. One major area where you can use them is in Ordnance Survey work.

You may need to draw a sketch map from an Ordnance Survey map to show one element of the landscape. For instance, you might be asked to show the relief and drainage of an area. You should concentrate only on those aspects when you draw your map. It should not contain any information about settlements, farming or anything not related to relief and drainage. As with all sketch maps, you should give it a border, in this case the required grid lines, and you should complete it with a careful key and title. An example is shown in Fig. 3.19. Figure 3.20 shows exactly the same area, but with information chosen to show only communications and settlement. To improve your ability in producing such sketch maps, select an Ordnance Survey map (either 1:50 000 or 1:25 000) and draw a series of sketch maps like Figs. 3.19 and 3.20 to show:

- relief and drainage
- communications and distribution of settlement
- the distribution of woodland

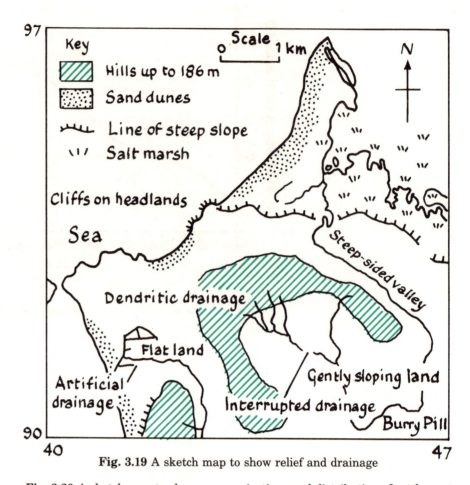

Fig. 3.19 A sketch map to show relief and drainage

Fig. 3.20 A sketch map to show communications and distribution of settlement

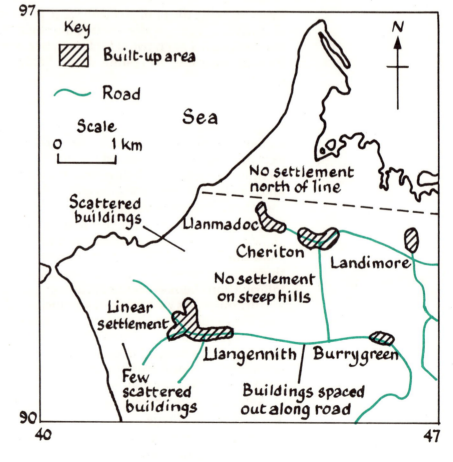

You may need to draw a cross section from an Ordnance Survey map when illustrating your coursework. You may need to draw a cross section in your Individual Study. The following list of points can be used if you are drawing a section:

1 Locate the two grid points between which you are drawing the section.

2 Lay the straight edge of a piece of paper between the two points. Make sure that you have the paper on the correct side of the line. Using the map with north to the top, if you need your section to be from west to east, lay the paper below the line of section with west on the left and east on the right. If the section needs to be from east to west, reverse the process (i.e. have the paper above the line).

3 Using a sharp pencil, mark on the paper the places where contours meet the edge, not forgetting to label them (Fig. 3.21).

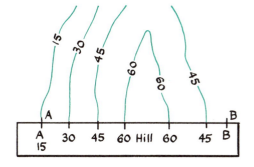

Fig. 3.21 Plotting contour lines on a section

4 On the graph paper or grid (if provided) draw a base line the exact distance between the two grid references. Your horizontal scale is therefore the same as that on the map.

5 Draw a vertical scale. This could be 2 mm to 10 metres for a 1:25 000 map or to about 15 metres for a 1:50 000 map. A smaller vertical interval will be necessary for a map of an area with a lot of hills.

6 Lay the straight edge of the paper along the base line and transfer the points you marked from the map on to the grid to give a graph of height (Fig. 3.22).

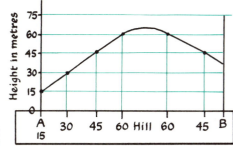

Fig. 3.22 Transferring points to a grid

7 Label the cross-section by drawing vertical arrows and printing carefully. (See Fig. 3.23 for a completed section from the Gower 1:50 000 map.)

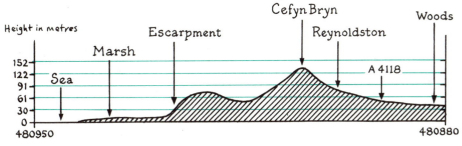

Fig. 3.23 A cross-section from the Gower 1:50 000 map

You should now be able to see how the relief shown by the cross-section helps to explain the distribution of settlement shown in Fig. 3.20. This is the sort of purpose for which you could draw a section. The sequence above describes how to produce a very accurate section. If you wanted a sketch section instead, you could follow the same sequence, but only mark off the high and low points, choosing perhaps every fourth contour to indicate slope.

Sketch maps can also be used to explain items on a much wider scale. An example might be the location of industry in the Ruhr area of West Germany. If you try to put this into words, you have to describe location, give the reasons for the choice of that location and say how it relates to everything else in the area. A sketch map is a shorthand way of saying all that. If used with a detailed key, you could deal with the entire question with a map. Sketch maps of this kind can be used to illustrate your coursework assessments and Individual Study. They can be drawn for the local area, a regional case study or even a world distribution. Figure 3.24 can be taken as a model for producing your own maps. These maps can also be used as convenient storage devices at the end of a case study. If you

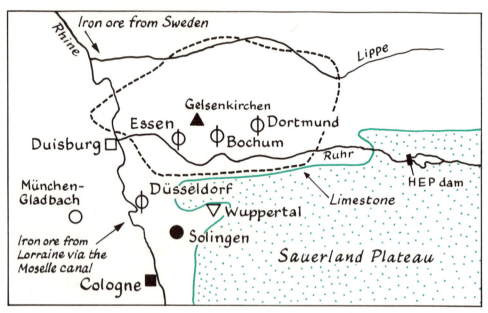

⌒‾⌒ Boundary of coalfield. Mining started in the south as open cast and adit mining. As reserves were worked out, operations moved north where deep mines are now working in the area of the Lippe valley

φ Iron ore and steel works use local coal and limestone, ore from Lorraine and imported ore from Sweden

□ River port. The Rhine and several canals provide cheap bulk transport

● Special steels (e.g. for cutlery)

■ Chemicals using coal, salt and oil

▽ Woollen textiles, formerly more widespread, using wool from sheep reared on the Sauerland Plateau

○ Cotton textiles, using skills developed in wool

▲ Aluminium smelting is one of the new industries helping to break the dependence on heavy engineering, coal mining and textiles. Others include car manufacture at Bochum and Cologne, electronics and assembly industries

High ground

Scale: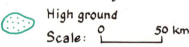

(You would not be able to put a scale on a map drawn from memory)

Fig. 3.24 Industry in the Ruhr area of West Germany

did not do so in the course of the case study, you can complete your own revision notes by producing a sketch map showing all the important information in that study.

A further method of simplifying notes, explaining relationships or illustrating processes is to use a flow diagram. The following passage of text has been simplified in the form of a diagram (Fig. 3.25). First of all, the key words have been underlined and then used to draw a diagram showing how they are linked.

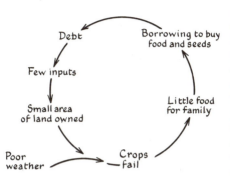

Fig. 3.25 The vicious circle of poverty

Small farmers in the Developing World are often caught in the vicious cycle of poverty. They have such a <u>small area of land</u> that only by very intensive farming can they produce enough food for their family. <u>When the weather is against them</u>, when there is too much or too little rainfall or when the temperature is too great, their <u>crops may fail</u> and they may therefore have <u>little to eat</u>. They then may have to <u>borrow from a money lender</u> in order to purchase food and seeds for the next year. In order to pay back the <u>debt</u> to the money lender, they may have to <u>sell some of next year's crop</u> or even pay him directly with the crop (a process known as share-cropping). This may well leave them short the next year and they will have to borrow again, making their position even worse. They may even have to sell some land.

Practise the technique by drawing your own diagrams to illustrate the following:

Many small rural settlements in Mid-Wales have been under pressure since the 1950s. Since that time, people have been leaving them to move to larger settlements where they have the chance of finding a job. What has happened is that traditional farming, which required more labour than the modern type, has declined. Some of the farms have been joined together to make large, often mechanized units, which need few workers. Former farm workers have moved away to find new employment, taking their purchasing power with them. This means that the local school, village shop and public house have also had to close, making the village even less attractive for the young people, who have therefore moved away. The villages have been in steady decline for these reasons.

✓ Checklist 6 Improving skills and techniques

Interpretation skills

1 Verbal

a) Write clear notes on the information you wish to interpret.

b) Underline the key words in your notes.

c) Use the key words as a list of terms to be interpreted.

d) For more complicated ideas, draw star diagrams or flow charts to show how ideas relate or stages fit together.

2 Written

a) Good note making is an important first step to interpretation.

b) Use photographs carefully. Always refer to them in the text.

c) Do not read more into a photograph than you can see.

d) Be prepared to draw diagrams or sketches to help with the interpretation of photographs.

e) Practise your technique by using photographs from books and magazines.

f) Spend time looking at graphs or diagrams before you begin to write anything.

g) In interpreting graphs and statistics, pick out trends, maximum and minimum points and ranges; then try to suggest reasons for each of these things.

3 Drawing

a) Practise drawing sketch maps from OS maps to show a theme (e.g. drainage, settlement, communications etc.).

b) Practise drawing sections from OS maps. You will not be asked to *remember* the technique, but it will help you to interpret maps more easily.

c) Practise drawing diagrams to illustrate descriptions.

Making up your mind

When you have collected a lot of information you will be in a position to say what conclusions you can come to about the results. You can also make judgements on them. This is true whether you have collected primary information from fieldwork or secondary information from text books, magazines etc.

The one golden rule you must follow is to make sure that you actually have the evidence for the conclusion you make. An extreme example might make the point better. You have collected weather records for February in your school grounds (near Liverpool) as a piece of fieldwork. They show low but fluctuating temperatures and a great variability of rainfall. You cannot say, however, that Februaries near Liverpool are always cold. Nor can you say that rainfall is variable when temperatures fluctuate over a month.

> *Always ensure that you have the evidence for any statement or conclusion that you make.*

You must make sure that your conclusions are not too sweeping and that they are relevant to the information you have collected. A much better conclusion from the example quoted would be that in February 1989 temperatures measured in the school field varied a lot. At the same time, rainfall amounts also varied considerably. Once you have established simple patterns like this, you can look for reasons behind them. In this case, a series of depressions during February would have led to changing cloud cover, the presence of different types of air (from the Arctic and from the warmer south) and therefore different temperatures and rainfall amounts.

If you are interested in judgements in this case, it might be that if there is a depression passing over the country in winter, you should take an umbrella with you if you go out! There is nothing very exciting here, but at least it follows on from what you have found in your fieldwork.

The skill of evaluating is the skill of drawing lots of information together and picking out patterns, which you can then explain. It is easiest to practise by using your class notes to begin with. At the end of a section of work on world population, for instance, you will probably have in your notes graphs, case studies, a model of population growth, population pyramids and general notes. You could use this information to test your skills of putting it all together. If you ask yourself, 'Is world population likely to continue growing at the same rate in the future?' and answer it by using all your information, you will be testing your skill of making conclusions. If you ask, 'Is there anything that can be done about it?' your answer will be in the form of a judgement and you should be aware that it is a personal judgement at that. After a while, having practised your skills in this way, you will be more used to the process and will be able to apply the same ideas to discussion, debate and role play exercises.

You should be aware that your conclusion is not the end of the story. It probably raises further questions. For example, in the case of world population growth, what will happen if growth continues at the same rate? What will happen when resources start to run out? Try also to be aware at all times that your conclusions are made in the light of the information you have available. What further information would you have liked in order to come to firmer conclusions?

Using models

In geography, maps are absolutely essential. They show in a simple way how things are set out in an area. Maps are simplifications of reality.

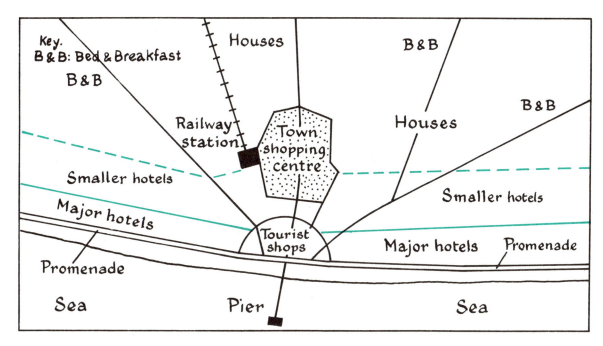

Fig. 3.26 A model of a British holiday resort

Depending on their scale, they miss out the minor twists and turns in roads, they use symbols to represent certain features and they select the information to show. In these respects, they are models of what is actually there.

Taking this idea a step further, it is possible to make a generalized map of what every large British holiday resort is like, for instance. Figure 3.26 is an attempt to do just that. It is not trying to say that if you go to Blackpool the sea will be to the south. What it is saying, though, is that the layout of the resort will contain the elements shown in the model and they will be arranged in roughly the same relationship. There are good reasons for this. When these towns grew, in late Victorian times, the railways were thriving and brought in industrial workers to stay in hotels and guest houses with the best views possible (along the seafront). The trains were steam powered and rather dirty, so they terminated a little inland from where the holiday makers were 'taking the air'. The focal point was the centre of the promenade, where a pier was often built. Try to think of reasons why the rest of the model is shown as it is.

Models are excellent for illustrating general ideas.

The idea of making a model, either as a diagram or in words, is one which you can use to clarify your ideas and to see the broader implications of your work. An example is shown in Fig. 3.27. A study had been made of the British iron and steel industry and of the Llanwern works, Newport, South Wales in particular. The simplified sketch map (Fig. 3.27(a)) had been drawn as a result. This was then used, along with the rest of the notes on iron and steel, to produce the model of the location of an iron and steel works shown in Fig. 3.27(b). This then served as an easy means of revision, a generalization which could be tested against other actual examples and as a way of looking at what would happen if various elements were to change, such as a decline in the international demand, a decline in coal production or an increase in the costs of labour.

Attempt to make summary models in your notes. These will be particularly useful in revision. Some areas from which you may be able to draw your own models, depending on your syllabus, include:

- the development of a port
- the way land use is arranged within a town
- the reasons for siting a factory
- the changing layout of a pit village over the years, etc.

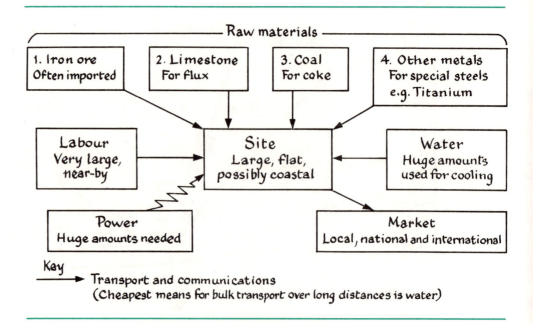

Fig. 3.27 a) The location of the iron and steel industry
b) Llanwern steelworks, Newport

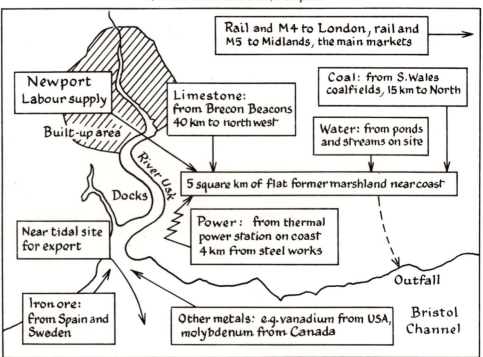

Skills of hypothesizing

'It's always wet on a Bank Holiday!'
That statement is of the type often heard in the United Kingdom. Many people blindly agree with it. In fact, it can easily be tested. The Meteorological Office holds records which will allow us to investigate the truth or otherwise of the statement. On investigating these records, we will at least be able to quantify the bare statement. Perhaps there is a 50 per cent likelihood of rain on Bank Holidays in August, but this hardly constitutes 'always raining'.

What we have just looked at is an **hypothesis**. This is a statement of which the truth can be tested by experiment. As a result, it can be accepted as it stands, rejected or modified. Hypotheses have a particular use in geographical investigation. The title of your Individual Study (discussed in Section Two) might be something like, 'What is the layout of land use around a town?' From this, we could make a number of hypotheses which could then be tested using fieldwork techniques. In this case, the hypotheses could be:

1 Land use changes away from the town.

2 The most valuable land uses are nearest the town.

3 Distance from the town is the only factor which affects the farmer's choice of land use.

In the first case, you could arrange to make a number of transects away from the town to test whether the land use changes. In the second you could sample land uses at various distances from the town and find, from various sources, how much return per hectare can be expected from those particular crops. In the third case, you can interview the farmers to see whether they can shed any light on your suggestion. All the statements can be tested by different fieldwork methods in order to establish their validity.

You will have ample opportunity on your GCSE course to use your ability to invent statements to test. Practise thinking in the required way by using the framework provided in Fig. 3.28 for not only the question provided, but also for others you come across during your course, and in particular when you are planning a major piece of fieldwork.

Question

How do the school buildings affect the microclimate?

Hypothesis one: There is a microclimate around the school buildings.

Method of testing: Use meteorological equipment to measure temperature, wind speed and wind direction around the buildings and away from them.

Hypothesis two: There is a relationship between the buildings and the microclimate.

Method of testing: Use statistical tests to look at such things as temperature increasing with closeness to buildings, wind speeds being higher where buildings are closer together and lower where they are sheltered.
(Continue for as many hypotheses as you have.)

Fig. 3.28 A framework for hypothesizing

Checklist 7 Improving evaluation skills

1 Ensure that you have the evidence for making conclusions and judgements.

2 Do not make your conclusions too sweeping.

3 Models are useful to simplify explanations – practise using them.

4 Practise *writing hypotheses* that you can use to test the truth of a statement. These will help with Individual Studies or Enquiries.

Data collection and recording

One of the major advantages of the GCSE examination is that it allows you to show what you are capable of doing on a personal basis. Fieldwork and Individual Studies are both ideal vehicles for you to show your abilities. Fieldwork can occur in many different forms. You may be given an exercise to complete in which you are told what to do step by step. Or you may have to plan every step of the exercise yourself. This section gives you a series of techniques you can use in order to collect information. In every case, the main uses of the techniques are looked at, followed by some hints on how to put them into practice. How to record information using the techniques is also studied.

There are two sorts of data you might collect. The first sort is **primary data** which is obtained by measurement, observation and questioning. Examples would be traffic flow figures, weather records and shopping surveys. The other type is **secondary data** which is obtained from books, photographs, magazines and censuses of various kinds. Examples would be production statistics, population figures and trade figures. You will need to collect both sorts during your course and this section will help you with where to look and how to manage the information.

Whatever the type of data you are collecting, you should not just collect for the sake of it. You should first have a clear idea of what data you need. One way to work out what it might be is first to make a list of the **objectives** of your study. As an example, let us suppose that you were wanting to investigate the sphere of influence of a small shopping centre. These might be your objectives:

The sort of data you collect will depend upon what you wish to do with it.

- To find out where shoppers at the centre live
- To find out how shoppers travel to the centre
- To find out how far from the centre it provides services

From these, the following techniques might be suggested:
For the first two points, questionnaires carried out in the shopping centre
For the third point, mapping the delivery areas of town centre shops, the local newspaper and major services (gas, electricity and post) organized from that centre. Information to be gained by asking in the distribution departments of large stores and the newspaper, and finding service area maps in the telephone directory.

When you write up your notes, remember to criticize your method. Was your data collected by the first method you thought of? Were there problems with earlier efforts? If so, how were they overcome? If you were doing the exercise again, are there any refinements you would include? All of these things are important in showing that you have understood the relevance of what you are doing.

You should always work as neatly as possible in the field because you may be asked to produce your original work, even though you will have written it up neatly.

In looking through the following pages, always try to make your choice of technique relevant by stating the objectives of your study first. Always save your rough notes and fieldwork records.

Methods of collecting primary data

Pedestrian/traffic counts

Main uses
- To investigate the movement of foot or vehicular traffic along a route
- To see how this traffic varies over time (See Fig. 3.16.)
- To find information on the use of routes in order to suggest changes to solve any congestion problems.

Methods of investigation

You first need to classify what you are measuring. For instance, in a traffic count, you need to divide the total traffic into groups such as cars, buses, lorries, motorbikes etc. You can then use these categories to devise an efficient collection sheet.

Next, you will need to decide on your sampling method. You cannot possibly measure traffic all day. You will have to count for five minutes or so at a time. There are also other decisions to make. Will you count both sides of a road or foot traffic going in one direction, for example? The best way to work out exactly where you are going to stand and for how long you are going to measure the traffic is to visit the proposed site of your study at roughly the time of day you were thinking of measuring and to conduct a trial count. This is a type of **pilot study**, which will help sort out any problems with the technique. The usual pattern of traffic along a road is as shown in Fig. 3.16, so this might help you to decide when to

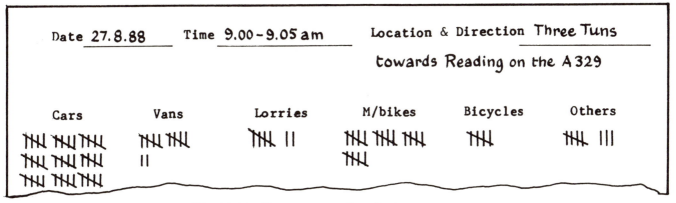

Fig. 4.1 A traffic survey recording sheet

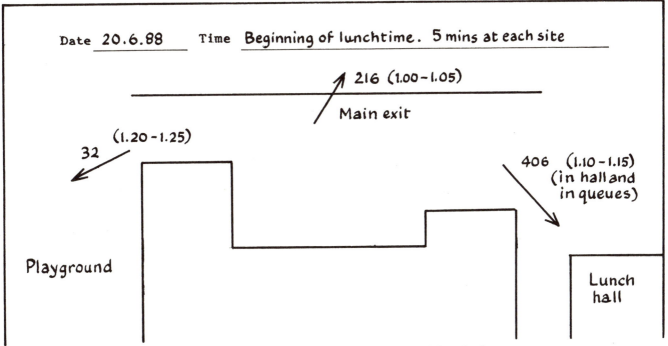

Fig. 4.2 Movement of pedestrian traffic around the school

Fig. 4.3 A hand-held anemometer

Fig. 4.4 A wind vane

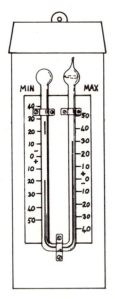

Fig. 4.5 A maximum and minimum thermometer

measure. If you are measuring the flow of pupils around the school at different times, you should observe the general pattern for a few days before deciding when to sample it.

Make sure, if you are conducting a traffic survey, that somebody knows where you are and at what times. Choose a spot which allows you to see what is going on, but does not put you in danger or obstruct others. Refer to the **safety rules** on page 23.

Data recording

A data recording sheet for a traffic survey might look like Fig. 4.1. One method of recording pedestrian flow around a school (if you are limited to counting by yourself) is shown in Fig. 4.2.

Weather and microclimate measurement

Main uses

- To measure the main elements for a place or an area over a given time
- To see whether changes occur over a small area
- To compare actual records with the weather forecast
- To see if there is any truth in weather sayings

Methods of investigation

The main elements and the instruments used for measuring them are as follows:

Wind speed Anemometer. The expensive hand-held version (Fig. 4.3) allows you to measure wind speed in metres per second, kilometres per hour, knots or Beaufort Scale. Make sure you always read off the same scale. Hold the anemometer away from you so that you do not interfere with the flow of the air.

Wind direction Wind vane or tissue paper. If you are measuring wind direction at one point, you can erect a wind vane (Fig. 4.4), which swings round to indicate the direction the wind is coming from. A westerly wind is a wind from the west; winds are always named by the direction they blow from. If you are measuring wind direction around a building, tear some very small pieces of tissue paper and drop them, marking the direction they travel on a base map.

Temperature Various types of thermometer. If you are measuring temperature at a given place, you can use a maximum and minimum thermometer. This should be read in the late afternoon by which time it will have had a chance to reach its highest temperature for that day. You should reset the indices by using the magnet provided as soon as you have read the temperatures (Fig. 4.5). It is important to take your readings at the same time every day, so choose a sensible time.

If you are measuring temperature differences around a building or built up area, you could use a Fahrenheit thermometer (since this shows finer divisions). You should note that you will only be given temperature readings in degrees Celsius in the examination, however. If a group of you are using thermometers for this purpose, do not forget to check them against one another to begin with. If one is found to measure a degree above the others, remember to take one degree from all the temperatures measured by that thermometer. Another instrument you could use to measure temperatures over an area would be the whirling hygrometer, which is mainly used for measuring humidity.

Humidity Whirling hygrometer (Fig. 4.6). This contains two thermometers. One has the bulb surrounded by a cotton wick which is saturated since the other end is immersed in a reservoir of water. It therefore measures the temperature of the air as it would be if it were completely saturated. The other thermometer measures the normal (or 'dry bulb') temperature. The difference between the two at the dry bulb

Fig. 4.6 A whirling hygrometer

Fig. 4.7 A rain gauge

temperature tells you how much water vapour there is in the air, or in other words the relative humidity. The hygrometer should be whirled round at arm's length for about one minute and the two temperatures read immediately.

Precipitation Rain gauge (Fig. 4.7). This is placed in an open site away from overhanging vegetation and emptied at the same time every day. The contents are tipped into a measuring cylinder whose diameter relates to the diameter of the rain gauge. You can not just use any measuring cylinder.

Other aspects of the weather or microclimate that you could comment upon through observation are the amount of **cloud cover** (usually expressed in eighths), the **cloud type** and the **length of time the sun shines**.

Data recording

The method will depend on the reason for your study. If you are collecting information from a fixed site, such as the school Stevenson Screen, you should ensure that you take readings at the same time each day, preferably in the late afternoon. You could use a recording sheet like that shown in Fig. 4.8. If you are recording the microclimate, you will have to record data at as many sites as you can around the buildings, garden or town being investigated. You will need to record the data as close together in time as you can so that you are measuring differences caused by the location and not by changing weather conditions. An example of how you could record the data (and hints to help you later with the explanation) is shown in Fig. 4.8 and Fig. 4.9.

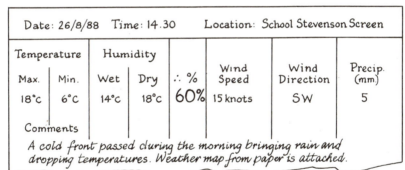

Date: 26/8/88   Time: 14.30   Location: School Stevenson Screen

Temperature		Humidity			Wind Speed	Wind Direction	Precip. (mm.)
Max.	Min.	Wet	Dry	∴ %			
18°C	6°C	14°C	18°C	60%	15 knots	SW	5

Comments
A cold front passed during the morning bringing rain and dropping temperatures. Weather map from paper is attached.

Fig. 4.8 A daily record sheet for weather data

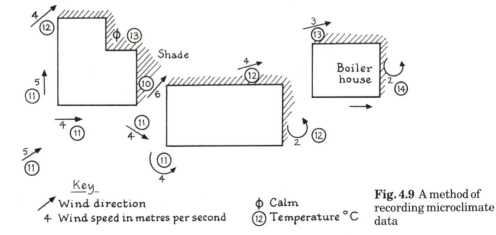

Key
Wind direction
4 Wind speed in metres per second
φ Calm
(12) Temperature °C

Fig. 4.9 A method of recording microclimate data

Vegetation and land use mapping

Main uses

- To show how vegetation changes with rock type, relief etc.
- To show how land use is arranged on a farm or over a small area
- To show how land use is arranged in a town
- To show whether land uses in the Central Business District are separate or grouped together

Methods of investigation

Vegetation mapping is best done with the aid of an Ordnance Survey 1:25 000 map and a Land Use Survey map (if available) for your area. This shows field boundaries, but also areas of woodland, marsh and rough land. A base map can be prepared from the OS 1:25 000 map. You can then use it to complete an up-to-date vegetation map by visiting the area and marking on it what you see. You will need a careful key to the map and you can plan most of this before you go into the field to do the mapping. Do not try to copy the woodland and marshland areas from a 1:50 000 Ordnance Survey map since this will not be recent enough, nor in enough detail for your purposes.

Land use maps can be completed in the same way as vegetation maps, but you will probably need some help with the identification of crops. Sometimes Land Use Survey maps are already available for your area but they will be out of date as land uses change frequently. You should ensure that you make your own map in the summer when the crops are most easily identified, or that you have a simpler key. This could be arable, pastoral, orchards etc. You should decide on the key to serve the purpose for which you are making the map. If you are making a map of land use on a farm, you will need a detailed key. If you are testing whether land use changes away from a market, you could use a more general key.

Another method of land use mapping, using a general key, is to complete transects away from some central point. This could be a town (in the case of farming land use) or a city centre (in the case of urban land use).

Data recording

A transect is simply a line drawn on a map along which you make some observations. You can decide on your transects by using random numbers to generate grid references, or you can take them in a number of directions away from the centre. As you travel along the transect (which need not be a straight line; it could be a road), you should note down the land use on one side. If you are travelling by bus, this is all you will be able to manage. If you are on foot, or on a bicycle, you can perhaps record detail on both sides. Again, you will need a general key if you are going to be able to interpret your results easily at the end. Figure 4.10 shows the results of a series of transects made in Reading and the possible interpretation of them. Figure 4.10(b) was drawn by using the field evidence provided by the transects together with the evidence from the 1:50 000 Ordnance Survey map of Reading.

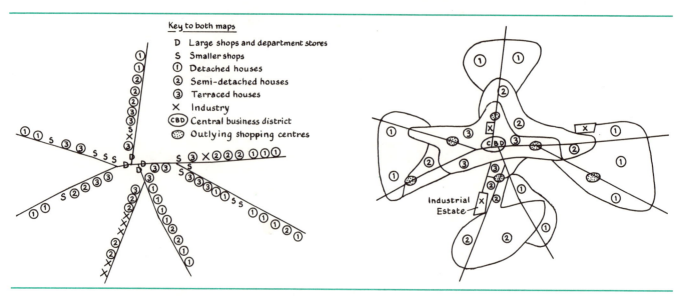

Key to both maps

D Large shops and department stores
S Smaller shops
① Detached houses
② Semi-detached houses
③ Terraced houses
X Industry
CBD Central business district
⬤ Outlying shopping centres

Fig. 4.10 a) Transects in Reading   **b)** The interpretation of the transects – a land use model of Reading

Soil investigation techniques

Main uses
- To determine the variations occurring in soil over an area
- To explain vegetation and land use distribution

Methods of investigation

If a good exposure of the soil can be found (or if a small pit can be dug), there is a simple descriptive exercise that can be completed. Make sure that you ask permission if you are completing such an exercise. Soil is commonly developed in definite layers (horizons) and these can be measured and described as shown in Fig. 4.11. Your description should refer to colour, depth, texture and moisture differences and allow you to compare between one soil and another. If you have an auger available, you could use it for the same purpose. An auger is a giant screw which can be worked down into the soil and pulled straight up to take a sample and allow you to suggest what the soil profile is like.

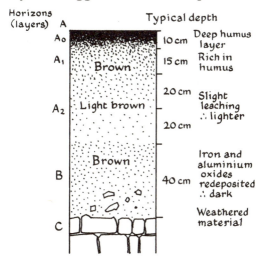

Fig. 4.11 A brown forest soil profile

Texture need not necessarily be described as broadly as we have seen so far. It can be related to certain properties of the different-sized particles. Sand of any size can actually feel gritty, either between the fingers or in the teeth. Silt feels silky. Clay can allow a small sample of the soil to be shaped into rings or rods. The possible mixtures of these three size categories can be shown on a triangular graph (Fig. 4.12). An explanation of how to read a

Fig. 4.12 Textural classes of soils

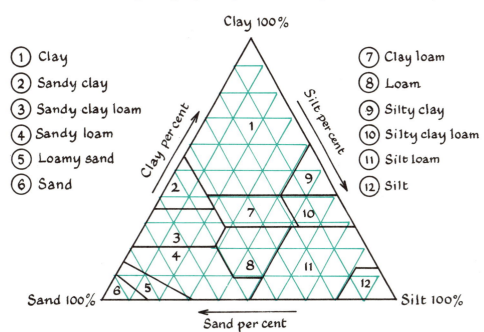

triangular graph appears on page 82. Each of the classes shown on the graph has its own distinctive properties, many of which can be identified by sight or feel. If you need to look in more detail at soil characteristics, you should refer to a text book on the subject.

The speed with which the soil allows water to infiltrate is an important feature and one which helps to explain the soil's fertility. It can be measured experimentally in the laboratory by using the method suggested in Fig. 4.13. This of course takes the soil out of its original context. Perhaps it has an underlying horizon which will not allow water through. It is therefore probably more important to know how the soil allows water to percolate without disturbing it. An experimental way of doing so is shown in Fig. 4.14.

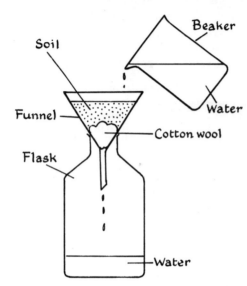

1. Set up the equipment as shown. Make sure the soil is dry.

2. Measure a quantity of water into a beaker.

3. Pour the water on the soil and time how long it takes to percolate through.

4. Repeat the experiment with different soils to get an idea of the variation in rates of percolation.

Fig. 4.13 Laboratory experiment to find how well soil allows water to drain

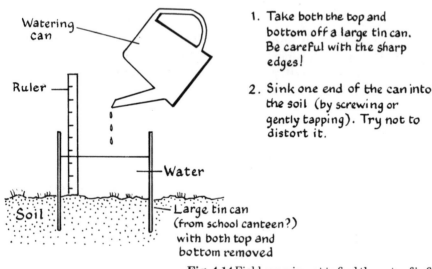

1. Take both the top and bottom off a large tin can. Be careful with the sharp edges!

2. Sink one end of the can into the soil (by screwing or gently tapping). Try not to distort it.

3. Place a ruler inside the can.

4. Pour in water up to a certain mark and time how long it takes for the water to reach a lower mark.

5. Either compare soils this way or carry on topping up the water until it stops sinking into the soil any more. This is when the soil has reached field capacity.

Fig. 4.14 Field experiment to find the rate of infiltration of water into the soil

Soil has a reaction known as its pH value. This measures how acidic the soil is. If the value is a number greater than seven, it is said to be *alkaline*. Seven is the value of a neutral soil and numbers less than seven mean that it is *acidic*. The value for any soil can be found by using a pH kit, or much more simply by using a pH meter. In the former case, a little of the soil is placed into a test tube and distilled water (*neutral pH*) added *just* to cover it. Universal Indicator is then added and this turns a different colour depending on the reaction. The colour can be matched against a chart. In the latter case, a small probe is pushed down into the soil and the pH value is read off on an electronic scale. This is far more accurate.

Data recording

When investigating soil, it is important that you clearly identify where each sample came from. If you are taking samples from an area, be sure to label them. For instance, you might take a sample for the percolation test referred to above. This could be put in a plastic bag with a small piece of paper noting where it was from. The location of the sample should also be marked on a sketch map. An example of such an exercise is shown in Fig. 4.15.

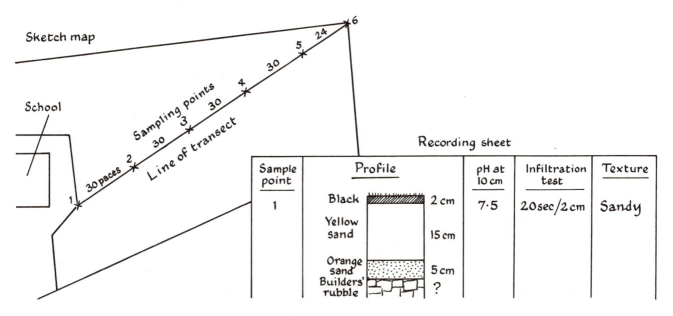

Fig. 4.15 Recording soil characteristics on a transect

River investigations

Main uses

● To measure the speed, direction and amount of flow of a river
● To relate these elements to the shape of the river channel
● To find the uses to which a stretch of river is put

Methods of investigation

Some collection of physical data can be dangerous! Remember the safety rules.

It should be stressed first of all that this sort of investigation could be **dangerous**. You therefore need to follow the instructions carefully and tell an adult exactly where and when you will be doing the work. It is also a good idea to do it with somebody else. All of the following exercises can only be completed in the way suggested in a shallow river with a firm bed, certainly not in a deep, muddy or fast-flowing river. Refer back to the **safety rules** on page 23. It should be stressed again that physical studies such as this are only in the spirit of GCSE if they are related to people. This study could be related to flooding, the potential use of the river, the siting of a bridge or some other environmental topic.

The river's speed can be measured in metres per second. In order to find this, measure a 10 metre stretch along one of the banks. Place a pole (a cane will do) at the start and finish of your section of river. Take an object which floats largely beneath the surface, such as a dog biscuit, ball or orange, and place it carefully in the river upstream of your first pole. As it drifts downstream and passes the first pole, start a stopwatch. As it passes the second pole, stop the stopwatch. Repeat the exercise about 10 times and find the average time taken to travel 10 metres. You can now work out the speed in metres per second.

The direction of the fastest flow within the river can be found by marking on a sketch map the path that the float takes. An example of such a map is shown at the bottom of the recording sheet, Fig. 4.17. The amount of flow is known as the **discharge** of the river. You have already found the speed of flow. Now you must find the cross-sectional area by measuring with a tape measure and a metre rule. First, measure at right angles across the river at the start of the section whose speed you have already measured. At every metre, or half-metre, depending on the width of your river, measure the depth with a metre rule and record it in centimetres.

Fig. 4.16 A fieldwork party measuring the Afon Gain in Wales

Repeat the process for the middle and end of the 10 metre stretch of river. You can now calculate the cross-sectional areas of all three sections by working out the areas of the triangles and trapezia in the way shown. (There is a short cut to this, which your maths teacher might explain to you.) You should then take the average of the three cross-sectional areas. This can be multiplied by the average speed in metres per second to find the discharge in cubic metres per second.

A sketch map of a section of river can be used to mark on the uses to which it is being put. You could locate the people fishing, walking, boating or bathing, the positions of waste paper bins, eroded banks, litter, boat hire stations etc., etc. You could make a study like this of the differences in use with different weather conditions or changes over a period of time. You might even be able to suggest a better management scheme as a result of what you have found.

Other members of your school staff may be able to help you with some investigations.

Data recording

A record sheet for plotting flow and shape of channel and a sketch map are shown in Fig. 4.17.

Field sketches

Main uses
● To show the form of a feature more accurately than it can be described
● To show complicated relationships between features
● To simplify the description of a landscape

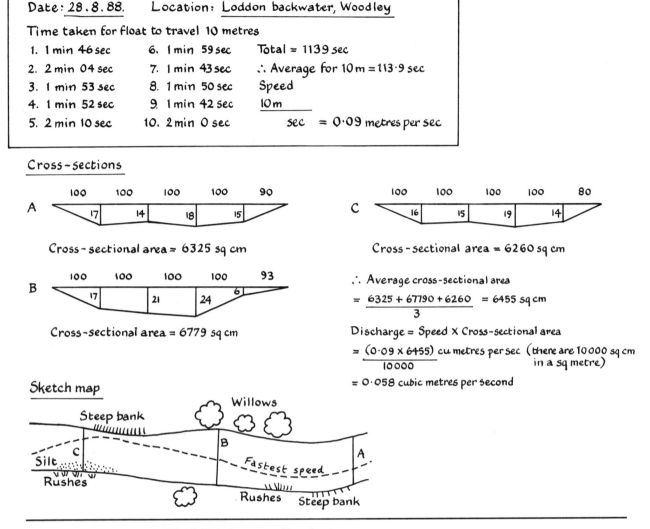

Date: 28.8.88.   Location: Loddon backwater, Woodley

Time taken for float to travel 10 metres

1. 1 min 46 sec   6. 1 min 59 sec   Total = 1139 sec
2. 2 min 04 sec   7. 1 min 43 sec   ∴ Average for 10 m = 113·9 sec
3. 1 min 53 sec   8. 1 min 50 sec   Speed
4. 1 min 52 sec   9. 1 min 42 sec $\dfrac{10\,m}{sec}$ = 0·09 metres per sec
5. 2 min 10 sec   10. 2 min 0 sec

Cross-sections

A   Cross-sectional area = 6325 sq cm

B   Cross-sectional area = 6779 sq cm

C   Cross-sectional area = 6260 sq cm

∴ Average cross-sectional area

$= \dfrac{6325 + 67790 + 6260}{3} = 6455$ sq cm

Discharge = Speed × Cross-sectional area

$= \dfrac{(0·09 \times 6455)}{10000}$ cu metres per sec (there are 10 000 sq cm in a sq metre)

= 0·058 cubic metres per second

Sketch map

Fig. 4.17 A river recording sheet

Methods of investigation

Field sketches can be used in nearly all aspects of geographical study. The main art of completing them is to simplify things without making them meaningless. A good field sketch should stand by itself without need for further description of what it shows, even though further explanation will probably be required.

The first thing to consider is whether there is any point in drawing a particular scene. Is it relatively easy to draw? Is it showing something sufficiently worthwhile? If so, then employ the following technique. Choose a vantage point which allows you as uninterrupted a view as possible. Draw the horizon, if relevant, and the main lines in the scene (for instance the shapes of buildings). At this point, check that the proportions and positions are about right. Do not worry over-much about absolute accuracy. It is a field sketch you are drawing, not a masterpiece! Select the main features you wish to show and make sure that you have sufficient detail to enable you to analyse them at a later stage. Label your sketch carefully. You can 'cheat' to a certain extent with field sketches, since you can draw them at a later stage from photographs you have taken, but this is useful probably only if you are drawing a landscape scene. A field sketch of an urban or agricultural scene completed from a photograph is probably a waste of time; you would be better annotating the photograph as shown in Fig. 4.20. You can also purchase postcards from which you can sketch, but do make sure that they are up-to-date scenes with all the features marked that actually exist!

Data recording

It is best to draw a field sketch inside a border since this allows you to make notes and put labels around the edge. A completed field sketch of a valley in North Wales is shown below together with the scene from which it was drawn (Figs. 4.18 and 4.19).

Fig. 4.18 Nant Ffrancon

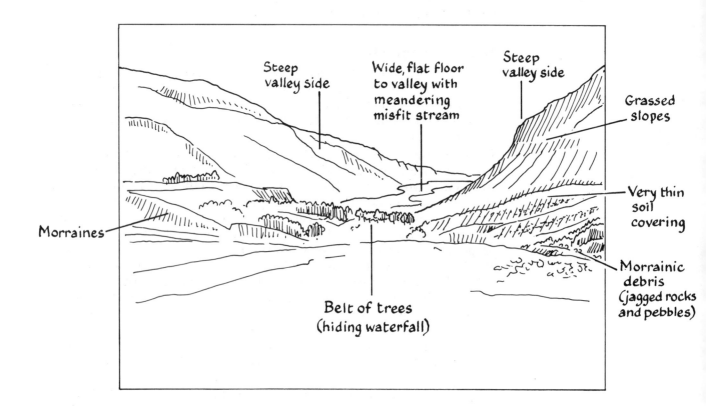

Fig. 4.19 A field sketch of the Nant Ffrancon valley

Photographs

Main uses

- To illustrate something too complicated to sketch
- To show how you completed a piece of fieldwork (method)
- To show progression over time (building, farm activities through the year)

Methods

You can use photographs that you have taken yourself, or postcards. In either case make sure that they actually illustrate something important and are not just there to make your work look attractive. Make a note at the time you take the photograph or buy the postcard to remind you why you chose that particular scene.

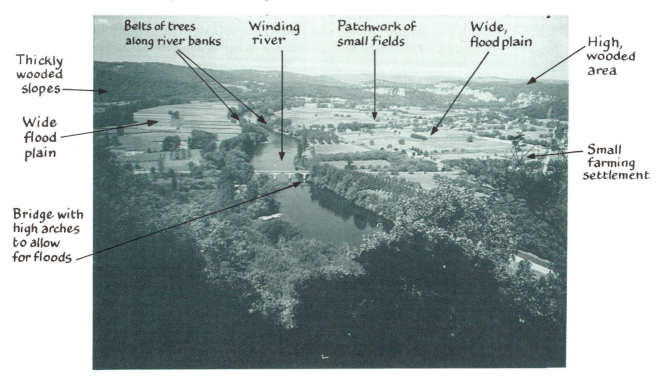

Fig. 4.20 An annotated photograph of a view over the Dordogne Valley from Domme

Data recording

When you present the photograph, remember to annotate it. It is no good just sticking the photograph in and giving it a title. Anyone could do that.

You, as a geographer, need to show that you appreciate what the photograph shows and you do this by labelling it carefully. Figure 4.20 gives you an example of how a photograph should be used.

Questionnaires

Main uses

- To question people at a certain location
- To ask for information from people from a large area that you are unable to visit
- To obtain details from somebody who is difficult to contact during the day
- To gain a body of opinion about a particular topic

Methods of investigation

A questionnaire should be as short and as relevant as possible. It should not ask for possibly embarrassing detail and it should be capable of easy interpretation. In other words, you need to determine exactly why you are asking the questions before you do just that.

You might be questioning people to investigate the sphere of influence of a shopping centre or store. If that is the case, those people will be in a hurry and will not wish to answer lots of questions. What do you need to find out? You would need to know where they live in order to be able to draw a map of the sphere of influence at the end of the fieldwork. You would need to know how they arrived at the centre or shop so that you can explain the sphere of influence. You might like to know their age and sex in order to be able to analyse your results better. These are examples of things that you can work out for yourself. If you ask, 'How old are you?' you could expect that many of the people would just go on their way without answering any more questions. Instead, you could have a predetermined list of age groups which you would tick according to your estimate of the person's age.

If you are delivering questionnaires to houses for later collection or if you are leaving them with managers at factories, for instance, you could ask for more detail than when conducting a questionnaire face to face, but the golden rule is never to ask anything that you would not be comfortable answering yourself.

The introduction to your questionnaire is absolutely vital, as is your reaction to people you are questioning. A good way to start is to say why you are doing the work and lead as quickly as possible into the first question. An example might be:

> Good morning. I am collecting some information to help me with my examination work in geography. Would you mind answering a couple of quick questions please? . . .
> Could you tell me how you travelled to this shop today? . . .

and so on. It may be easier for your interviewee to look at the questionnaire and for you to fill it in together. If you are rejected, do not answer back or be impolite. Just say, 'Thank you,' and move on to the next person.

Only use a questionnaire if an adult knows where you are and has checked what you are going to ask first.

'Good afternoon. My name is Norman Law and I am carrying out some work for my geography exam. Would you mind answering a few questions about shopping please?'

Respondent: MALE/FEMALE

Under 16	35–50
17–25	over 50
26–35	

(You simply circle the details which apply **after** the person you have been asking has gone away, just in case they see you and you get it wrong!)

1 Can you tell me in which postal area you live?

Reading	Woodley	Shinfield	Pre-selected so
Earley	Southcote	Caversham	that you can
Lower Earley	Whitley	Whiteknights	tick the one that
Tilehurst	Coley	Emmer Green	applies. Saves time.

OTHER (Write in) _____

2 Can you please tell me where you normally go to purchase
    bread?   records?   furniture?

_____

3 How frequently do you shop for each item mentioned?
    bread?   records?   furniture?

_____

4 How do you travel to each of these places?
    bread?   records?   furniture?

_____

'Thank you very much indeed for your time. You have been most helpful.'

Fig. 4.21
A shopping questionnaire

If you are considering delivering questionnaires for people to fill out in their own time, try to talk to them as you deliver the forms. If this is not possible, write a letter giving your details and those of the school, so that it gives every appearance of importance. Tell the person when you will call back for the completed questionnaire and stick to the time. Of great importance is the fact that you should let someone know where and when you are going back for the completed questionnaires. Try to call in daylight, or if that is impossible, get an adult to help you. Better still, of course, design your questionnaire to be used face to face.

Try to make the questions as easy as possible to answer. If possible, list out common answers so that you can just tick them rather than having to write out complete answers. An example of a simple questionnaire aimed at finding where people from a particular area of a town go to do their shopping is shown in Fig. 4.21.

Perception studies

Main uses
- To see whether different people view things in different ways
- To see whether people's ideas of space change over time
- To judge the success or otherwise of developments

Methods of investigation

'Perception' means the way someone looks at or understands something. A different kind of questionnaire can be used to obtain people's views of geographical phenomena. If you write two opposite statements on either side of a page, people answering the questions (respondents) can mark where they believe the truth lies. You can give each point a numerical value as shown in Fig. 4.22. If you then ask a number of people to respond to the questionnaire, you can work out the average values given by

This area of the Lake District is . . . . . .

X	X Applies 1	Neither really applies 2	Y Applies 3	Y
beautiful	✓			ugly
lovely	✓			crowded
peaceful	✓			noisy
historic		✓		modern
exciting		✓		boring

The overall value for this person's response is 7 (a total of the values for each tick). Each individual answer can be compared numerically against someone else's. You could have a five point scale instead of a three point scale.

Fig. 4.22 A perception study

different groups, such as teenagers, young parents and senior citizens. You can also use this method to test people's reactions to developments, for example new buildings. If the buildings are well known, you can ask people to react to them from the name itself. If not, a photograph could be used and people asked to mark their response on a table such as the one shown in Fig. 4.22. If you have a number of statements, one under another, you can join the points that mark the response of one person, or one group of people, to achieve their perception 'profile'. This is shown in Fig. 4.23.

The City of Norwich . . . . . .

	Agree strongly 1	Agree 2	Neither agree nor disagree 3	Agree 4	Agree strongly 5	
. . . is boring			X			. . . is exciting
. . . is modern					X	. . . is historic
. . . has few facilities			X			. . . has lots of facilities
. . . has little to do			X			. . . has plenty of entertainments
. . . is ugly			X			. . . is beautiful

Fig. 4.23 A perception profile

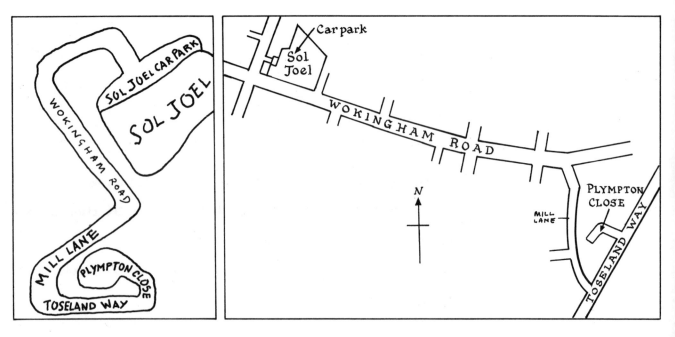

Fig. 4.24 a) An area as perceived by a ten-year-old   b) The actual map of the road

If you ask someone the way to the town centre, they will give you directions based on what they know of the area. Younger people may signpost turnings by pub names and older people by public buildings (the library, for instance). If you ask them to draw a sketch map of the journey there, they will often draw it according to how they travel there. People with cars will see it as not very far away. People who travel by public transport will see it as much further. In addition, perception of scale varies greatly with age. Younger people tend to think of the object at the end of the journey and give it undue importance in terms of scale. They also concentrate greatly on the journey itself and ignore landmarks to the sides of the route. Figure 4.24(a) is a sketch map made by a ten-year-old who was interested in playing football at Sol Joel Park. The actual map is reproduced next to it (Fig. 4.24(b)). The youngster ignored the fact that Wokingham Road did not start just where Mill Lane joined it and he made Sol Joel's rather larger than it should be! People's perception of journeys greatly affects whether they will make them or not. You could ask different people to draw sketch maps for you of particular routes and analyse the results.

Slope measurement

Main uses

● Measuring slope angles in land use, landform, coastal or transect work

Method of investigation

The piece of equipment required in order to measure slope angle is known as a **clinometer**. The manufactured version, which you might be able to borrow from your school, is basically a spirit level mounted on a pivot, with a device like a protractor for measuring angle. If you cannot borrow one, you can easily make one for yourself. Figure 4.25 is a diagram from which you should be able to make one.

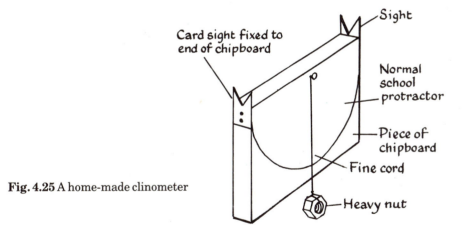

Fig. 4.25 A home-made clinometer

In order to use the clinometer, get a garden cane and stick it into the ground. Stand right next to it and paint a very clear mark (with luminous paint, for instance) at exactly the same height as your eyes. Now go to the slope you are going to measure. Stick the cane in and walk 10 paces up the slope. Use the clinometer to view back down the slope to the mark on the cane. Hold the cotton against the protractor with your hand when the nut has stopped swinging and read off the angle. Note it down and, with a second cane, mark the position from which you took the reading. Retrieve the first cane, walk a further 10 paces up the slope and repeat the exercise. Do not forget that the angle will be measured to one side of the 90-degree line on the protractor if you are viewing uphill, to the other side if you are viewing downhill. If by any chance the slope is not continuous, but has a dip in it, remember to mark this on your records. It may be a good idea to draw a sketch of the slope before you leave it.

Data recording

A typical recording sheet is shown in Fig. 4.26. Note that space has been left for additional notes and a sketch of the slope has been drawn.

Site	Distance from last point	Angle	Comments
A	0	3	next to river
B	10 paces	10	wooded slope
C	10 paces	12	wooded slope
D	10 paces	5	field
etc.			

Sketch of slope

Fig. 4.26 A slope recording sheet

Checklist 8

Data collection technique or equipment	Examples of application
Pedestrian/Traffic counts:	To measure flows over a given time
Weather records:	
Anemometer	Wind speed
Wind vane	Wind direction
Thermometer	Temperature
Whirling hygrometer	Humidity
Rain gauge	Precipitation amount
Land use:	
Land use mapping	To show pattern and change over time
Land use transects	To sample land use over a large area
Soil investigations:	
Soil profile description	To show layers in the soil
Soil texture description	To show differences over an area
Infiltration rates in soils	To compare drainage characteristics
River investigations:	
Measuring flow	To compare rivers or to relate to landforms
Measuring channel shape	To relate to flooding potential
Description:	
Field sketches	To describe complicated relationships
Photographs	To illustrate method or give example
Sampling:	
Questionnaires	To establish a body of information
Slope measurement:	
Clinometer	To show the angle and shape of a slope

Methods of collecting secondary data

Use of libraries

Main uses

- For finding other people's work on your subject, including their views
- For obtaining other people's primary data (census data, planning documents, etc.)

Methods of investigation

You will no doubt be familiar with the services offered by your own school library. Similar services are offered at the local library and the central library in your nearest large town. Apart from *lending* books, however, libraries have several other purposes. You can use them as *reference sources*. If you yourself cannot find the information you require, you can ask the librarian, who will either direct you to the correct section of the library or show you the **index**. Some libraries have subject and author *indexes* in which you can search for what you want. Some have computerized indexes to help you find things more quickly. In the case of larger libraries, there may be a *'key word' index*, so that if you look up the word 'census', for instance, you are directed to all the different census figures held in that library.

Libraries contain much more than just novels!

Some libraries have past copies of newspapers on *microfilm*. They probably have all the *planning documents* relevant to your county. If your central library does not have these, the library attached to your County Council building will have. To locate them, ring your County Council, ask for the library and then ask for any specific *statistics* you may require. If the librarian is convinced by the importance of your case and is not too busy, you might even be given the information over the phone.

Libraries attached to local colleges or universities may also be able to help you. Sometimes if you contact one library and ask for information, the librarian will direct you to one of these other sources if it is not available there. Most libraries have collections of *local information*, on the local settlement for instance. There may be *photographic* records as well. There is almost certain to be a *map* department from which you may be able to purchase photocopies of old maps for your study. Finally, the larger libraries will contain *periodical* sections where you can refer to well-known magazines such as *The Geographical Magazine* and *Geo* as well as less well-known ones such as *Ekistics* and *New Zealand Geographer*.

Larger libraries may have the results of the national 'Domesday' survey of 1986 on laser disc.

You cannot be expected to know all the services your library offers, nor can you be expected to find the information straight away. The best thing to do, therefore, is to **ask the librarian** for assistance. If you go about it in the right way, you will be given every help and you will be able to find your information much more efficiently.

Local newspapers

Main uses

- For tracking the history of local developments such as major building schemes, park provision, the local road network and industrial changes

Methods of investigation

Your local newspaper will have its own library. This will contain cuttings which are filed in folders according to subject. Sometimes, however, it is not clear how a cutting should be filed and it would need to be cross referenced in another file.

There are probably also original photographs in the files. You will need to make an appointment to go and view the files, which may be got out ready for you if you know exactly what you are looking for. The telephone number for your local newspaper will be in your local telephone directory.

If you are interested in more recent items, you may not need to go to your local newspaper office, but instead you can follow the development of a topic from week to week in the current papers. Keep cuttings of the items that interest you, but do not forget to date them carefully. If you are using more than one source, also mark the name of the newspaper. Do not forget that the letters page often gives you another view of the topic.

National newspapers

Main uses

- To illustrate coursework assessments or special studies with relevant, up-to-date information
- To obtain information on case studies covered in coursework
- To obtain weather maps

Methods of investigation

You can use national newspapers to collect cuttings on current events. Many newspapers also have special reports from time to time and sections on industry, the climate, farming and many other topics. The colour sections of some Sunday newspapers can be particularly useful as well. If you keep cuttings, remember to file them carefully and label them with date and source.

Some libraries keep past copies of national newspapers, sometimes on microfilm. *The Times Index* is an index to all the *Times* group newspapers. It is released monthly and annual bound issues will be filed in the library. It has a name index and you will be able to find the date, page and even the column where any particular article appeared. You can use this index to find what you are looking for, before using it to find the correct page on microfilm.

The British Humanities Index is a similar index for selected references from *Geography, Geographical Magazine, The Guardian, The Daily Telegraph, The Times* and, more recently, *The Independent*. A document you could use if you wanted to trace the development of a topic over a period would be *Keesing's Contemporary Archives*, which has a summary of recent events concerning a particular topic or area.

Television and radio

Main uses

- To obtain background information on topics covered in class
- To get different views on controversial subjects
- To keep up with current events which might affect areas you have studied in class
- To help understand that geography is about the real world

Methods of investigation

You can obtain a tremendous amount of information in readily remembered form by listening to radio or watching television. It is probable that you watch videos of specially recorded schools programmes in class. Probably also, when you have been ill and away from school, you have seen very useful programmes which you have not later seen at school. There is not enough time for your teacher to show you all the programmes which may be of use to you. You could get together with a few friends and scan the radio and television pages for anything which looks useful. You might even be able to have space on your geography room notice board to share this information. If you are lucky enough to have a video or radio-cassette player, you can swap recordings of useful programmes. With particularly useful case studies, you should be able to make notes, using the methods referred to in Section Three.

Magazines

Main uses
- As for national newspapers and television and radio
- To obtain detailed information on specialist subjects

Methods of investigation

'Wise use of television and radio can be very beneficial and you will probably enjoy it more than book work!'

There is a very large number of magazines published weekly or less frequently. You can find out just how many by visiting a local branch of a large stationery chain and looking at the magazine racks. Your local library will also have a periodical department. It will have an index of titles and if you are confused about where to look for any particular information, you can ask the librarian. Again, remember to label and date any photocopies or cuttings you save.

Other sources

There are many other sources of free information which might help with a particular study you are making. The Embassies or High Commissions for different countries can be located by looking at telephone directories (usually for London) which are kept in your nearest main library. If you cannot find the information there, ask Directory Enquiries or the librarian.

Various companies publish Public Relations information which they make available on request. Addresses of the largest companies can be found in a directory called *Kompass*, which might also give you valuable information.

Censuses are of particular use to the geographer. The national census for the UK is published every 10 years, but estimated figures are always available for intervening years. The census information is available at different scales, right down to parish or ward (a small unit of local government) level. Censuses relevant to your area are kept in your local library, but others are kept in main libraries.

Figures on matters of world importance are available from publications such as *The United Nations Year Book*, various statistical publications from the EEC, the various charities such as Population Concern, and the year books and monthly reports of the major banks.

On a more local level, local maps and information on local property are available from estate agents. Various local shops will be able to give you details of delivery areas. The local telephone directory (plus *Yellow Pages*, *Thomson Local* and similar publications) all have details of delivery areas and service areas, including maps.

Parish magazines and the local leaflets delivered by various political parties might give you an insight into local issues and the way different people react to them. The planning department of your civic centre may also have information on local issues. If you are looking for a particular source of information, ask your teacher or another adult, your school librarian or the local librarian. You will find that they are only too willing to help someone who is trying to help themself.

Checklist 9 Sources of secondary data

Source of data	Example of application
Libraries	To obtain other people's views on a topic
Local newspapers	To trace the history of a local issue
National newspapers	To follow issues of world importance
Television ⎫	
Radio ⎬	To relate class studies to the 'real' world
Magazines	To obtain detailed information on specialist subjects
Embassies, High Commissions etc.	To get detailed information on countries
Censuses	To find population statistics
Parish magazines	To get local views on issues

Presentation of data

Good presentation is essential to obtain a better GCSE grade.

No matter how carefully you have collected your information, you will not get the full benefit from it unless you present it as clearly as possible. There are many ways you can present your data, so you will always have to ask yourself which is the best method for the particular information you have. You can, of course, simply describe what you have found. If you are doing this, refer to the notes on written presentation in Section Three. You have already been told how you can practise your drawing skills in that same section.

In this section, the following pages give you a range of presentation techniques. For each one, an idea is given of the most relevant uses. You are also given a step-by-step guide for producing each sort of map or diagram. Remember that your maps and diagrams should be drawn carefully, not rushed, using the right equipment and in the right conditions, with plenty of room on a desk, for instance. A list of the equipment required is given in Section Two. In your fieldwork and Individual Studies, your examiner will be looking for a wide range of techniques to illustrate the work.

Tables, graphs and charts

The presentation of tables

Main uses

● To give the results of your survey, especially if there are very large numbers of records, prior to selecting some for drawing diagrams, graphs etc.
● To give a summary of analysis, for instance lists of Rank Orders
● To show the working for some statistical techniques

Technique

The most important thing to remember when presenting tables is that the headings must be clear so that the person reading the table will be able to see what it represents without continually referring back to the text. The table should have a clear title and be referred to in the text. Tables are used in the working of Spearman's Rank Correlation and various other statistical techniques referred to later in this section. The one illustrated in Table 5.1 shows the results of a piece of rural settlement fieldwork carried out in West Yorkshire. Table 5.1 was later used to establish a hierarchy of settlement in the area. The table has been drawn so that the most frequently found services occur in the first few columns. The settlements are arranged in order of population size. Arranging it like this helps you to see patterns more easily.

Line graphs

Main uses

● Climate graphs and weather records
● To show values over a given time (e.g. production and population data)
● To allow the visual interpretation of trends

Services

	Pop.	Church/ chapel	Pub	General store	PO	Primary school	Butcher	Hardware	Clothes shop	Hairdresser	Supermkt.	Secondary school	Shoe shop	Bank	Hospital
Otley	12 000	√	√	√	√	√	√	√	√	√	√	√	√	√	√
Bramhope	3 500	√	√	√	√	√	√	√	√	√	√		√	√	
Pool	2 000	√	√	√	√	√	√		√	√				√	
Huby	1000	√	√	√	√										
Pool Bank	500		√	√	√										
N. Rigton	420	√	√	√	√	√									
Weeton	150	√		√	√										
Leathley	100	√													
Arthington	50	√	√	√	√										
Braythorn	30														
Castley	30														
Clifton	30	√	√												
Farnley	20	√				√									
Stainburn	20	√													
Newall	20			√											

Table 5.1 Services and population of some West Yorkshire settlements

Techniques

The most important thing to do before plotting a graph is to try to picture the finished article. You could even go as far as to draw a sketch of what the graph might look like when you have plotted it. Generally, you will have the dates or times of readings on the x-axis (horizontal) and the readings themselves on the y-axis (vertical). You need to choose the scales for these axes correctly. In order to do so, you should find the maximum and minimum values. If you are drawing the graph on A4 paper, work out how much you can allow for the y-axis, remembering that the graph will need a title and the axis will need to be labelled. Now that you have the range of the values and the maximum height available for the y-axis, you can decide on the scale. You should have a feeling already about what the values show. If you think they show a dramatic rise or major fluctuations, you can decide on a scale which reflects this. If there is little change over the period measured, do not choose a scale which makes it look as if there is!

The x-axis should always show an even progression. If you have taken readings for 1, 2, 3, 4, 5, 6 and 10 o'clock, your x-axis will need more than seven divisions, even though you have only seven readings. There should be the correct spacing between them, as shown in Fig. 5.1. When you have plotted your figures, join the points with a line drawn with a hard, sharp

Always have an idea of what the finished diagram will look like before you start drawing it neatly.

lead pencil. You should draw ruled lines if the graph shows totals with no gradation between one and the next. Annual production figures are an example. On the other hand, temperatures should be joined with a smooth line since they do not change dramatically in real life. They change smoothly from one hour to the next. If you are drawing a smooth line on a graph, do so by keeping your hand inside the curve. You may need to turn the graph upside down in order to draw it like this, but if you do so, your elbow will act as a sort of pivot, or pair of compasses, to allow you to draw a smoother line.

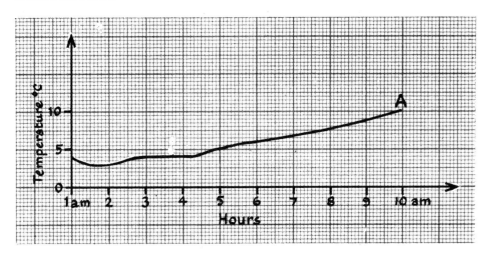

Fig. 5.1 Temperature records for one morning

Upgrading your presentation

You could annotate your graph so that you can refer to it more easily in the text. For example, you could label the maximum temperature on Fig. 5.1 as A. In your text you could say, 'The maximum temperature (point A on Fig. 5.1) was 10°C and was reached at 10 o'clock.'

One way of spotting a trend on a line graph is to re-plot the values as moving means. The mean is the total of all values divided by the number of readings (this is often called the **average**). For instance, if you have values for the first three years, find the mean and plot the value for the central date. Next, use the values for the second, third and fourth year and repeat the exercise. The process is shown in Fig. 5.2. You now have means plotted for the second and third years. Carry on plotting by each time dropping the first of the three years you have just handled and adding the next one on the list. You can use this technique for any number of years, though odd numbers are easiest to handle. Three-year, five-year and seven-year moving means are the most common. You can also use it for any time sequence of data. It does not have to be years.

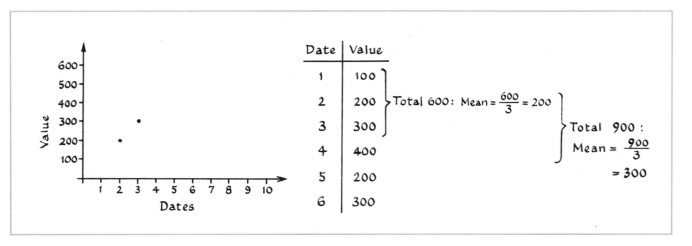

Fig. 5.2 How to calculate and plot moving means

Pie charts

Main uses
- To show how a total is composed of parts
- To compare between the totals of more than one set of figures
- To compare the importance of constituent parts of a total

Techniques

A pie chart is a circle (representing the total) divided into segments (representing the constituent parts). If you are just interested in the relative importance of parts (subtotals) making up a total, you can draw your circle any size. The divisions of the circle are found by working out the following:

$$\frac{\text{angle required}}{360°} = \frac{\text{size of subtotal}}{\text{size of total}}$$
$$\text{Thus angle required} = \frac{\text{size of subtotal} \times 360°}{\text{size of total}}$$

Example

Let us suppose that the total of a ship's cargo was 1000 tonnes. This was made up of 400 tonnes of coal and 600 tonnes of limestone. Working out the size of the segments:

$$\text{Angle required for coal (400 tonnes)} = \frac{400 \times 360°}{1000}$$
$$= 144°$$

$$\text{Angle required for limestone (600 tonnes)} = \frac{600 \times 360°}{1000}$$
$$= 216°$$

(The second one has been worked out even though you could just take 144° away from 360°. This is purely for checking purposes.) In many cases you will have to round totals to the nearest whole number. Make sure in this case that the total still equals 360°. You will notice that in the sums above, $\frac{360}{1000}$ appears in both. A short cut would therefore be to work this out (0.36), and to use this to multiply each subtotal to find the required angle. Figure 5.4(a) shows the pie chart drawn for these figures as well as a way in which the presentation can be improved.

If you want to show two or more totals by using proportional pies, draw them both so that their radii are drawn using the square root of the totals. This is because the area of a circle is πr^2. If you want to make the circles proportional, you can ignore π since it occurs in the formulae for all of them, and just find the square roots to use as the radii. Work out the angles for any constituent parts exactly as before. An example is shown in Fig. 5.3.

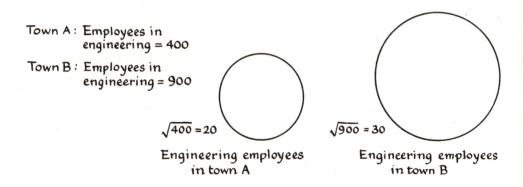

Town A : Employees in engineering = 400

Town B : Employees in engineering = 900

$\sqrt{400} = 20$

Engineering employees in town A

$\sqrt{900} = 30$

Engineering employees in town B

Fig. 5.3 Proportional pie charts showing relative totals

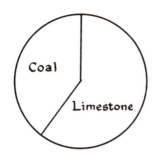

Fig. 5.4 a) A pie chart illustrating the composition of a ship's cargo

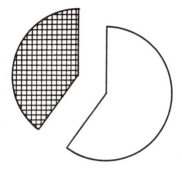

b) A highlighted pie chart showing the importance of coal in the ship's cargo

Upgrading your presentation

You can locate pie charts on a map of the area to which they refer. If you are describing one constituent part of a total, you can redraw the pie chart with that segment 'removed' from the circle and highlighted in a colour, leaving the rest of the circle blank (Fig. 5.4(b)).

There are computer programs which allow you to generate pie charts, but unless your printer is a very good one, you will not achieve a very good shape. It is likely to be somewhat stepped in appearance. You can use computer plots to trace a good copy.

Bar graphs and divided rectangles

Main uses
- To show precipitation figures on a climate chart
- To illustrate several sets of data
- To compare data by superimposing one set on top of another
- To draw population pyramids
- To show how a total is composed of constituent parts

Technique

Bar graphs are drawn using a vertical scale decided upon in the same way as for line graphs. There is no x-axis as such. Instead, the bars are drawn next to one another, using the same base line, so that their heights can be read off the vertical scale.

Population pyramids are two sets of bar charts arranged so that the centre vertical line acts as the base line. Bars are drawn horizontally to either side of this line so that the net result sometimes looks like a triangle – but hardly a pyramid (Fig. 5.5(a)).

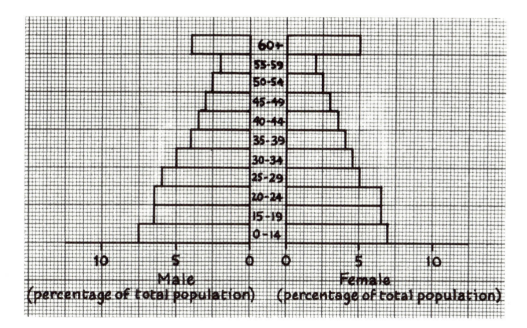

Scale: 1 cm = 100 tonnes

Fig. 5.5 a) A population pyramid
b) A divided rectangle showing the composition of a ship's cargo

Bar charts are often drawn so that one set, perhaps for one year's figures, are superimposed on another. They can be coloured differently so that they are easily separated visually.

Divided rectangles show the same sort of information as pie charts and there is less chance of making a mathematical error. The whole rectangle represents the total. The length is then divided so that the constituent parts are represented by each of the sections. If the bar is drawn 10 cm long (100 mm), then 14 per cent of the total is represented by 14 mm (Fig. 5.5(b)).

Upgrading your presentation

The bar charts can be located on a map to illustrate both the figures obtained and where they were achieved. Bar charts can be made to look more impressive by giving them a '3D' effect as shown in Fig. 5.6. Computer-generated bar charts and divided rectangles can be very effective.

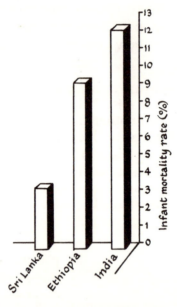

Fig. 5.5 Enhanced bar charts showing infant mortality rates in three countries

The bar charts are drawn as normal but given a 'solid' appearance by drawing them like this. Your Design or Arts departments at school will help you if you wish to use this technique of presentation.

Maps   Dot maps

Main uses
● To show the distribution of items on a base map

Technique

On a base map of an area which shows administrative divisions, or at least a few points by which things can be located, dots can be located to represent one or more occurrences at that place. For example, if you had recorded several hundred shoppers in a shopping count, you would not be able to give one dot for each, or the entire map would soon be covered. Each dot would therefore have to represent several records. Make sure that dots are drawn using even pressure and do not try to make the symbols small circles, as it will prove impossible to keep them the same size. Fig. 5.7 is an example of a dot map.

Upgrading your presentation

Sometimes you can draw the dots in different colours, for males and females perhaps. This could give you more to say when you come to the analysis.

There are some very good computer programs for drawing dot maps.

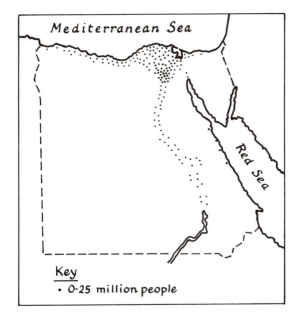

Fig. 5.7 A dot map showing population distribution in Egypt

Choropleths

Main uses
- To show distribution
- To show densities

Technique

A choropleth shows the density of something by using shading or colour. The lowest density is generally shown by shading well spaced out or by the lightest colour. The greatest density is shown using closer shading or the darkest colour. The best choropleths use a gradation of shading or

Fig. 5.8 A choropleth map showing the percentage of Italy's total workforce working in industry

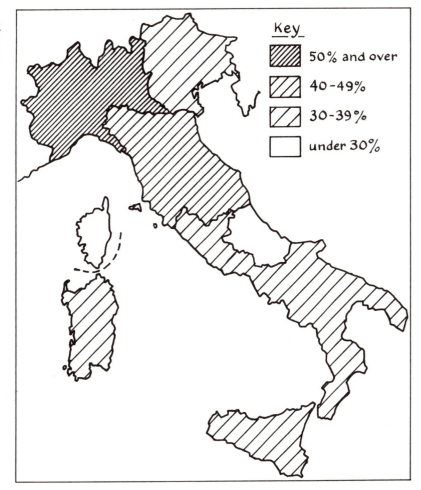

Key
- 50% and over
- 40-49%
- 30-39%
- under 30%

colour so that you can see at a glance how the distribution is arranged. The most important step to take to ensure that the map actually shows something useful is to divide the data into correct classes in the first place. You can use an even scale, a logarithmic scale or even a random scale, so long as it covers the data and divides it into distinct classes. Your geography or mathematics teacher or a friendly senior pupil would be able to help here. Figure 5.8 shows a completed choropleth map.

Upgrading your presentation

Use a well-thought-out colour scheme when shading your map. If you have six classes, shade them so that they give the best possible visual impression of increasing density from one class to the next. Your art teacher will be only too pleased to help you select the scheme for your shading. You should try to keep the colours in the same 'family'. For instance, white, yellow, green and blue are closely related and give an impression of increasing density. Reference to atlas choropleth maps will give you a good idea of what colours to use.

Again, computers can be used to generate very effective choropleth maps, so long as the base map is not too complex.

Sketch maps

Main uses

● To locate any case study in coursework, fieldwork or Individual Studies

Techniques

Sketch maps should be drawn at as large a scale as possible to show some particular attribute of an area. You will probably base the map on Ordnance Survey maps, which you can obtain either from school or from a large bookshop. (If there is a particular map you require at a particular scale, you may have to order it, so leave yourself time to obtain it.) You can also obtain useful base maps from estate agents and from Tourist Information Centres. You may, however, have to base your map solely on fieldwork.

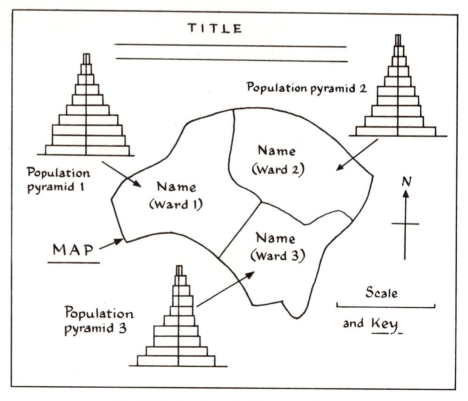

Fig. 5.9 A plan for a sketch map or diagram

Plan out your sketch map in rough before attempting to complete it properly. Your rough sketch could include an idea of where on the paper your drawing would go and where there would need to be room for labels. This will avoid the frustrations of drawing a beautiful diagram, only to find that you either cannot finish it properly with the labels or that you spoil it by adding them.

Figure 5.9 shows how a plan might look.

Next, make sure that your finished sketch map will fit into your paper by devising a scale. It is usually best to draw a frame on your paper within which to construct your map. Let us suppose that a stretch of the River Blackwater in Essex has been surveyed and that the length of that stretch is 50 metres. The river is fairly straight. In order to fit this on to a piece of A4 paper, which is 298 mm along its long side, and in order to leave room to draw a frame, you could assume that the frame will be 250 mm long. This will make your scale easier, for it will mean that as 250 mm represents 50 metres, 10 mm represents 2 metres.

Now construct your sketch map carefully using a soft pencil and pressing lightly. Once you are sure the shape is right, you can go over it with a sharp hard pencil and remove any construction lines with a rubber. You should now show the characteristics of the channel by using suitable symbols and shading. If you use symbols, try to make them recognizable. You could use variants of the Ordnance Survey symbols, for instance triangles showing a shallow cliff, or stylized versions of what you are trying to illustrate, for example the lily pads shown on Fig. 5.10. Whichever you use, you will need a key which will appear if at all possible on the same sheet as your map. If you use any extra labels, make sure you leave enough room for them, or place them on the page where there is no other information and locate them with arrows. All these examples are shown in Fig. 5.10 which is an example of a sketch map drawn from field data. Colour may be added to make the feature clearer and the sketch easier to understand.

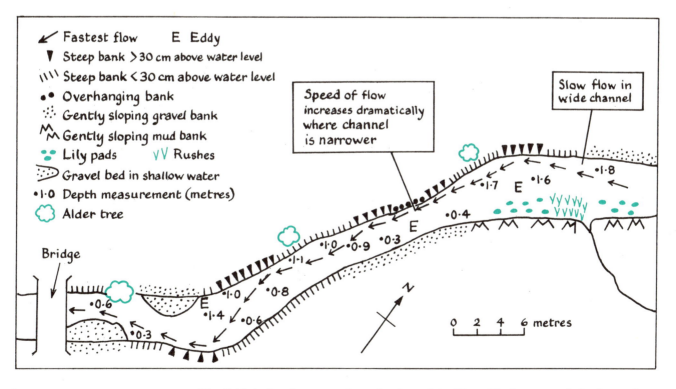

Fig. 5.10 A sketch map to show the flow of the River Blackwater and the form of the channel

Another example is of a sketch map for a shopping street in a small settlement. The information was collected using an Ordnance Survey 1:2500 map which was annotated with the types of shop during the fieldwork. In presenting the information on a sketch map, all the data from the original map which did not relate to the topic being studied was omitted. The final map therefore simply shows the buildings, the purpose for which they are used and a key. The problem with this map is to show the type of use clearly whilst not covering it with labels. A simple abbreviation key has been used where necessary to overcome this (see Fig. 5.11). Colour shading would be equally effective.

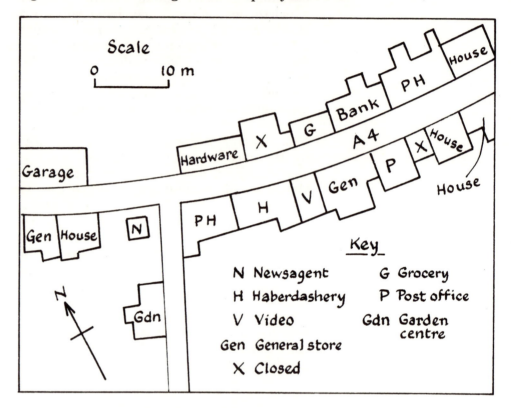

Fig. 5.11 A sketch map to show the building use in the main street of a village

Statistics

Flow lines

Main uses

- To illustrate the results of traffic censuses
- To show movements from one place to another
- To compare movements in two or more periods of time

Technique

A flow line is simply a long bar chart. It is drawn in the same way, by widening the route of a road, for instance, according to a scale of so many millimetres per so many cars. Usually the route of a flow line is 'straightened out' to make it easier to draw. The direction of movement can be shown by forming one end of the bar into an arrow as shown in Fig. 5.12. One of the lines has been left in skeleton form so that you can see how it has been drawn. All the lines on a flow line map should be shaded in the same colour since they all show the same thing.

Upgrading your presentation

If you produce two different flow lines for the same route at different times, drawing them on tracing paper will allow you to superimpose them and see how the two relate.

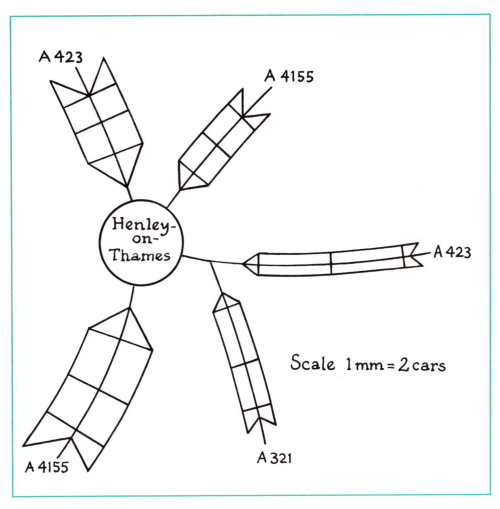

Scale 1mm = 2 cars

Fig. 5.12 A flow line diagram showing numbers of cars travelling towards Henley-on-Thames between 11.30 and 11.35 on 30.8.88

Scatter graphs

Main uses
● To see how two variables change in relation to one another
● To enable the relationship between two variables to be picked out

Technique
If you have data which shows two sets of readings, for example distance from a river and the number of days per year irrigation is needed, you can plot the results on a scatter graph. This has two axes, one for each set of variables. Points are plotted with dots at the coordinates given by the

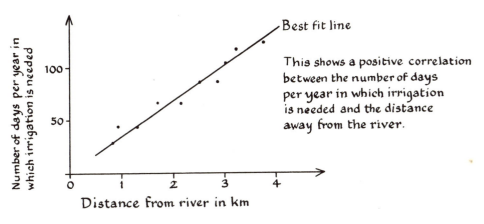

Fig. 5.13 A scatter graph

readings. If a clear trend emerges, for example if there is a band of dots from lower left to upper right (as in Fig. 5.13), you have established a positive link (correlation) between the two sets of figures. You could sketch a line which describes this relationship and this is known as the 'best fit' line or regression line. One is shown in Fig. 5.13. If the best fit line runs from top left to bottom right, however, a negative correlation is shown. This would mean that as one set of values increases the other decreases. It should be noted that neither correlation means that one set of values changes *because of* the other. It only suggests a link for further investigation.

Upgrading your presentation

This is one of the best applications of the computer for graphics, since it will draw the accurate best fit line without you being involved in masses of calculations.

Triangular graphs

Main uses

● To illustrate how totals are composed of three elements, e.g. sectors of employment, soil texture, composition of traffic on a road etc.

Technique

An actual triangular graph is given as Fig. 4.12. Points would be plotted on this graph using the three sides of the triangle as the base lines. The lines on the graph and how to use them are illustrated in Fig. 5.14. Points should be plotted with a dot in the same way as for a normal graph.

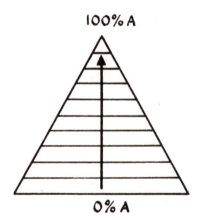
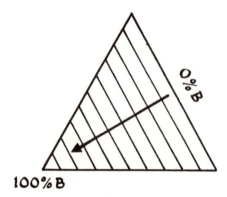
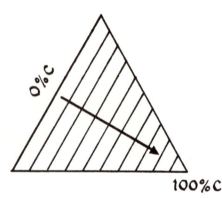

Fig. 5.14 How to read triangular graphs

Upgrading your presentation

A triangular graph can be used to decide on classes of information, in much the same way as the soil texture classes have been shown in Fig. 4.12. You can plot your data on the graph, spot any clustering or grouping of points and place a border around these points to highlight their relationship.

Statistical techniques

Main use in general

● To analyse data and pick out relationships or patterns

Specific techniques

Percentages

These can be used to reduce large sets of data to manageable numbers. They are also very useful when you have different production figures or employment figures for different years. In saying how many per cent of the production total is composed of farming produce in two years, for example, you will be able to see whether or not the change in farming production has been in proportion to changes in the rest of the production figures. Percentages are useful in displaying the responses to a questionnaire.

Spearman's Rank Correlation

This is a technique used to spot the relationship between two sets of data. A visual way of spotting relationships has been described above under *scatter graphs*.

The scatter graphs shown in Fig. 5.15 show three possible relationships and the Spearman's Rank number which describes them. Thus, a perfect positive correlation is given by a Spearman's Rank value of $+1$, a perfect negative correlation by -1 and no correlation by a value of 0. The method of finding the value is described below.

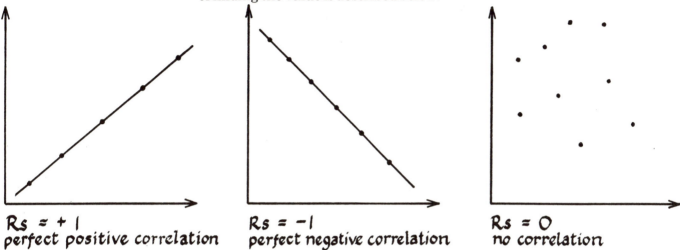

Rs ≈ + 1
perfect positive correlation

Rs ≈ −1
perfect negative correlation

Rs ≈ 0
no correlation

Fig. 5.15 Values of Spearman's Rank Correlation Coefficient and what they mean

The formula Spearman's Rank Correlation Coefficient is R_S and

$$R_S = 1 - \frac{6 \times \Sigma d^2}{n(n^2 - 1)}$$

where d is the difference in rank between one set of values and another and n is the number of readings. Σ means 'the sum of'.

Park	Area of park in hectares	Rank of area	No. of visitors	Rank of visitors	Difference between ranks	Diff. in ranks ^{2} (d^2)
A	15	1	3200	1	0	0
B	5	2	500	3	−1	1
C	2	3	650	2	+1	1
D	1	4	120	4	0	0
E	0.6	5	15	5	0	0
						$\Sigma d^2 = 2$

NB *This is just an illustrative example. To make it meaningful, you really need more than 10 sets of data.*

Table 5.2 To show whether there is any relationship between the size of a park and the number of visitors it attracts

Worked example

If you have two sets of readings as shown in Table 5.2 Spearman's Rank would be worked out as follows:

$$R_S = 1 - \frac{6 \times 2}{5 \times (25-1)}$$
$$= 1 - \frac{12}{120}$$
$$= 1 - 0.1$$
$$= +0.9$$

Only use statistics if you are sure what you are doing. They will only impress if they are correctly applied.

What it means

This indicates a very strong positive relationship between the size of park and the number of visitors. It *does not* prove, however, that because a park is large, it attracts more visitors. It simply suggests that there is some sort of relationship worthy of further study. In fact, the reason for the relationship might be that larger parks have more facilities for young children. It is not directly their size, but how that size is used which explains the relationship.

Location quotient

This technique allows you to compare the share of a total in one area with the share in another. For industry (one of its main uses for the GCSE), it is worked out as follows:

ILQ (industrial location quotient)

$$= \frac{\left\{\dfrac{\text{Number employed in one industry in one area}}{\text{Number employed in the same industry in the whole region}}\right\}}{\left\{\dfrac{\text{Number employed in all industry in one area}}{\text{Number employed in all industry in the whole region}}\right\}}$$

Worked out for the data in Table 5.3, the missing ILQ is:

$$\text{ILQ for engineering in town A} = \frac{2000/25\,000}{6000/1\,000\,000}$$
$$= \frac{0.008}{0.006}$$
$$= 1.33$$

Town	Employed in engineering	Total employed	ILQ
A	2000	6000	1.33
B	1000	6000	0.67
C	500	6250	0.32
D	200	4000	0.2
E	50	3500	0.06
Country as a whole	250 000	1 000 000	

Table 5.3 Engineering employment in five towns – statistics for industrial location quotients

If the ILQ is more than 1 the industry has a higher concentration there than in the rest of the country. A figure of 1 shows average concentration and a figure of less than 1 shows that industry to be less concentrated in

84

that area than in the rest of the country. In this case the location quotient for engineering in town A shows a marked concentration there.

Location quotients can be used for incomes, house prices or anything which is distributed unevenly across an area and for which figures are available. You might be able to think of a novel use for the idea.

Further notes

The methods of presenting photographs and field sketches have been referred to above. It is very important with all these techniques that you give every diagram or map a **title**, a **key** and a **north line** or **compass direction** if applicable. It is equally important that you refer to the diagram in the text by saying something like, 'As shown in Fig. 5.9 the shape of a river's channel and the characteristics of its flow are closely connected.' Never draw a map or diagram just for the sake of it. Make sure that you have a good reason for doing so!

 Checklist 10 Presentation techniques

Technique	Example of application
Table of figures or presence/absence	Comparing services in settlements
Line graphs	Plotting change over time
Pie charts	Showing totals and subtotals
Bar graphs	To show comparative totals
Divided rectangles	Showing totals and subtotals
Dot maps	To show distribution
Choropleth maps	To show distribution and density
Flow lines	To show volumes of movement
Scatter graphs	To show how variables correlate
Triangular graphs	To show composition of totals
Statistical techniques	For showing detailed relationships
a) Percentages	
b) Spearman's Rank Correlation	
c) Location Quotient	
Sketch maps	To locate case studies
Photograph presentation	To illustrate examples

Some examples of student investigations

Having looked at all the individual techniques of investigation, analysis and presentation, we can now consider how they all fit together into student investigations. This will be done by looking at a few examples of typical GCSE projects, or Individual Studies as they might be called. Each study described below has been successfully used by students in the past to show what they had learned, could understand and could do.

Study 1   What is Reading's sphere of influence?

Objectives

To draw a map of the area that could be called Reading's sphere of influence and to explain why it is that size and shape.

Data collection

The student started by getting a map of the service area for the Gas Board whose area is based in Reading. He found the name of the Gas Board in

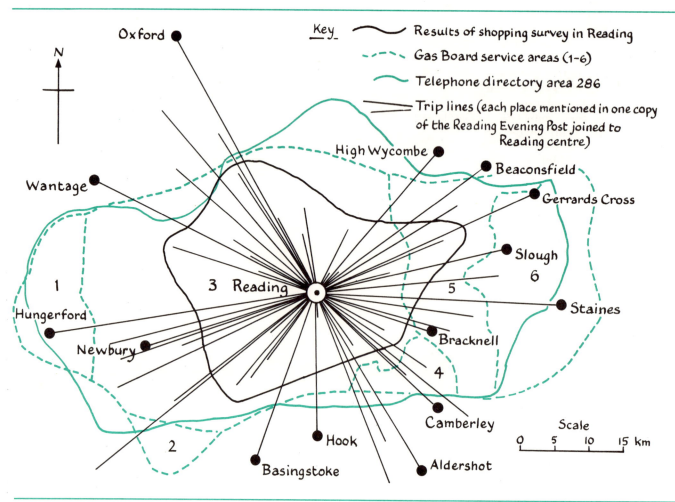

Fig. 6.1 The sphere of influence of Reading

the local telephone directory. The area served by the directory itself was also shown. In fact, there were several other maps of spheres of influence shown in the directory that he could have used, as well as this one. He decided not to because he wanted to show that he could use other sources of information. He therefore conducted his own shopping survey in the town centre, making a list of the places where the people who answered the questionnaire lived. The Gas Board area, the telephone directory area and the shopping survey results are shown in Fig. 6.1.

The student also used one copy of the *Reading Evening Post* (the local evening paper). He marked on a copy of the local map the location of every place mentioned in the paper. On his final map, he joined each of these locations to Reading town centre, giving another method of representing the sphere of influence. Again, this is shown in Fig. 6.1.

In this way, the student used both primary and secondary data. He also used different methods of data collection.

Data presentation

The student drew a map using two techniques of showing the sphere of influence, which are boundaries and trip lines.

Analysis

Having drawn the sphere of influence map (Fig. 6.1) the student compared its shape with the actual map of the area (the 1:50 000 map). He found that the 'sphere' was elongated from west to east.

This is the direction of the River Thames and its valley. Communications follow the river and as a result it is easier to get to Reading from the west or the east. To the north are the chalk hills known as the Chilterns and to the south are hilly gravel areas which are thickly wooded.

He also suggested that the actual size of the sphere of influence is governed by competition from surrounding towns such as Basingstoke, Oxford, Aldershot and High Wycombe.

Study 2   How do the functions of two small settlements differ?

Objectives

● To compare and contrast the services, industry and transport of two villages in West Yorkshire

Data collection

The student drew sketch maps of two similar-sized villages from 1:10 000 OS maps. These were carefully labelled to show details of site. They were photocopied at the outline stage so that they could be used as field maps for collecting information on services, industries and transport. This was completed by field mapping. The secondary information, the map, was therefore used to collect primary data. A visit to the County Council offices gave the student all the information she needed on employment in the villages. Copies of the parish magazines for both villages gave her further vital information. Traffic counts were conducted in each village and a short questionnaire was used in both to get an idea of shopping and travel patterns.

Data presentation

Good copies of the village land use maps, bar graphs of employment statistics and pie charts of the preferred shopping locations were drawn (Fig. 6.2). An analysis of the questionnaire results involved comparing answers given by people living in one village with those given by people living in the other village. This was presented in the form of two tables.

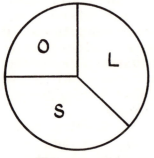
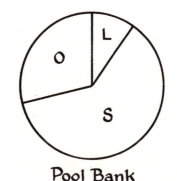

Bramhope   Pool Bank

Key

L Prefer to shop for groceries in the local shops

S Prefer to shop for groceries in the supermarket in Otley

O Shop for groceries elsewhere

Fig. 6.2 Shopping patterns for two West Yorkshire settlements

Analysis

The differences in all the topics under investigation were highlighted. These were then examined in more detail by comparing sites, looking at distances to competing centres and referring to public transport timetables.

Study 3   What is the best position in my back garden for locating a rotary clothes line?

Objectives

- To investigate microclimate differences in a garden for a practical purpose

Data collection

A plan of the back garden was drawn from accurate measurements. Copies of this were used to collect information on wind speed and direction, amount of direct sunlight, temperature and humidity differences at certain times. A questionnaire was completed (Fig. 6.3) amongst 20 current users of rotary lines, to find what they considered to be the most important factors in locating a rotary clothes line.

Data presentation

Maps were drawn for each of the microclimate elements measured. The results of the questionnaire were tabulated and illustrated with bar charts. A 'model' of the perfect location was drawn.

Analysis

The model was compared with the maps of the actual site. A compromise solution was found which did not lead to the line being located in an obtrusive site.

Study 4   Plan and carry out a piece of fieldwork which involves counting numbers of cars or pedestrians

Actual title chosen How does the location of Waitrose affect the pedestrian flow in Woodley shopping precinct?

Objective

- To draw maps of pedestrian traffic in Woodley precinct and to establish whether the Waitrose end is more heavily used.

Fig. 6.3 Questionnaire

My name is _____ and I am collecting information to help me with my Geography GCSE enquiry. Would you mind answering a few quick questions please?

1. Do you use a washing line to dry clothes? Y/N (if N, thank and close. If Y, go to 2).

2. Could you please tell me how important you think the following factors are for the location of a washing line?

Location of line...	Very Important	Important	Ave.	Unimportant	Very Unimp.	D/K.
In a windy area						
In direct sunlight						
Away from overhanging trees						
In an open area						
Near the kitchen door						
On a paved area						

Others (write in)
Thankyou for your help.

Data collection

A large plan of the precinct was drawn, based on the original shopping centre plan, with recent additions mapped by measurement. This was used to establish sampling points at which pedestrian counts were carried out. These lasted for five minutes (counting both directions). They were carried out on a number of days, both when the supermarket was open and when it was closed. A short questionnaire was used to find out whether people were mainly attracted to shop there by Waitrose.

Data presentation

Several sketch maps were drawn (Fig. 6.4) to show pedestrian movement at different times. Graphs were drawn highlighting the differences between total numbers of pedestrians near the supermarket and those further away.

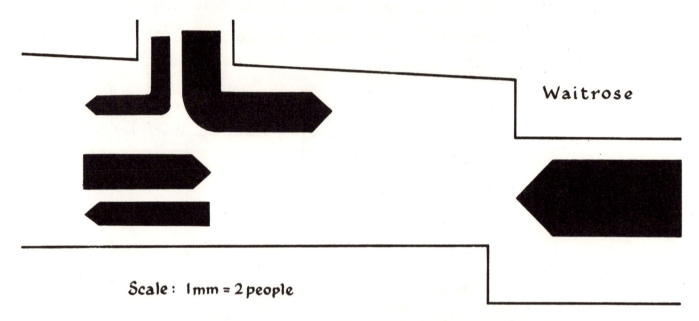

Scale: 1mm = 2 people

Fig. 6.4 A flow line diagram to show the movement of people in Woodley precinct between 09.00 and 09.05 on Monday 22 August

Data analysis

The importance of Waitrose to the attraction of customers to the other businesses in the precinct was established. The routes to and from the car parks were seen to be the most frequently used in the precinct.

How your work will be marked

A good proportion of the marks for the GCSE examination come from coursework. You can check in Appendix 1 to see exactly how large a percentage of the marks in your syllabus will come from this source. The types of work you will have to complete vary from syllabus to syllabus and you can check to see exactly what will be required of you in Appendix 1. The rest of your marks will come from an examination at the end of the course. The marking of these two sections is done in a different way and it is useful for you to know the system so that you can check your progress and know what to expect.

There are differences between the ways in which examination groups conduct the marking of coursework, but the following is one common pattern used. You will be given the results of your coursework shortly after you have finished each item. Your teacher will mark the work to a mark scheme that has been passed by someone appointed by the examination group. (This person is known as the **moderator**.) As mentioned before, you must not expect to get one mark for every correct point you make. Answers are marked for the understanding they show, your knowledge, expression of your point of view or for the skill you have exhibited in the answers. The teacher has to record the marks gained by everyone and a sample of the school's work is sent off when requested by the moderator. In this way, both the accuracy of the marking and the standard as opposed to those of another school are checked. Probably you will be given back your coursework assessment to look at before the sample is sent off. You will have a chance to see why you got the marks you did, so that you can improve the next time. The marks for all the required coursework may be known before the examination and you should have a reasonable idea of how you are doing before that. The overall grade for coursework is made up of a balance of knowledge, understanding, skills and values (as shown in Table 1.1). At about the same time as you are taking the examination, there will be a meeting of all the teachers involved in the marking of coursework. At this meeting, they will check again that the marking has been fair to individuals and fair between schools. After that, the results from each school will go to the examination group.

There are many checks to ensure that you are given full credit for all the work you do.

The examination will be marked by 'external examiners'. These people will not know any of the individuals and probably none of the schools they mark. They will mark just as before, based on the knowledge, understanding, skills and values expressed by each candidate. There is a chief examiner who checks that the standard of marking by each of the examiners is a good one. This might be done by re-marking a selection of scripts from one examiner. In this way, checks are built into the system all along to see that a fair result is achieved.

If candidates fail 'without good reason' to submit part or all of the fieldwork they will not be given a grade. If you are ill *for any reason*, make sure that you get a doctor's certificate to prove that you were unable to do the work. It may cost you something, but it could be very valuable.

In the end, the marks for the coursework and the marks for the examination are put together and the decision is made about where the grade boundaries come. It is impossible, therefore, to say that a particular mark is what you must aim for to achieve a grade C. Even at this point, if there are any glaring differences in what a candidate achieves in coursework and in the examination, the case is looked at again. If you had been suffering from some illness at the time of the examination, you will have had a medical certificate sent in, which might count for you in a situation such as this. If you arrived late at a school and did not take a particular assessment, this will not count against you, as it will not if you missed one for any other good reason. Your teacher has to submit a 'Special Difficulty' form, which tells of any problems like this and they are all taken into account. The levels of competence you will be expected to reach for certain grades are shown in Table 2.3. Simply, the more abilities you show, the better you will achieve. Many of these abilities can be improved by practice and many hints have been given in this book about how you can do this.

So there it is! There is really no need for fluffy animals on the examination desk. If you work at your skills and techniques during your course in a planned and orderly fashion, you should have no need of lucky charms. Make your own luck by putting in the correct amount of effort in a well-organized way.

 Checklist 11 How your work will be marked

1 Coursework marks are gained gradually throughout the two years.

2 Your teacher will mark several assessments during your course.

3 You will be told how well you are doing and will have the chance to learn from any mistakes you have made.

4 The marking at one school will be checked against the marking at another.

5 The final examination will be marked 'externally' (i.e. by people other than your teacher). Again, the standard of marking will be checked.

6 Marks for the coursework and examination will be put together to give your grade over the whole course.

Summary table of coursework

The coursework % will be achieved by submitting the following items:

	LEAG A	LEAG B	LEAG D	MEG A	MEG B	MEG C	MEG D	NEA A	NEA B* (Scheme 1 / 2)	NEA C	NEA D	NISEC	SEB	SEG A	SEG B	WJEC 0018	WJEC + MEG AVERY HILL
Value of coursework as a % of total	30	40	25	25	28	50	50	25	60 / 25	30	50	20	25?	25	40	20	40
of which knowledge recall	–	–	–	–	–	–	10	–	9 / –	–	8	–	–	–	–	–	8
... Understanding, application skills + values	11	16	7	5	10	23	22.5	8	24 / 8	15	27	Approx 10	–	10	20	8	14
... Practical skills	19	24	18	20	18	27	17.5	17	27 / 17	15	15	Approx 10	–	15	20	12	18
Coursework assessments	–	2	–	–	–	–	3	–	4	–	3	–	–	–	2	–	–
Teacher-planned enquiries	–	–	–	–	–	–	2 either TPE's	–	–	–	2 either TPE's	–	–	–	1	–	–
Individual study/ geographical enquiries	2	–	–	1 long or 3 shorter	–	2	1 or IS*	1	–	2	1 or IS	1	–	1	–	1	–
Coursework studies	–	–	–	–	–	–	–	–	–	–	–	–	–	–	–	–	3
Decision-making exercises	–	–	–	–	–	2	–	–	–	–	–	–	–	–	–	–	–
Fieldwork (✓ = compulsory)	✓	1	note-book	✓	note-book	✓	✓	(or ✓ sec)	–	(or ✓ sec)	✓	–	–	must be included in Geog. Enquiry	✓	✓	–

*The Individual Study can be a number of separate studies

* Two schemes

† Not available until 1990

At the time of writing all information about syllabus requirements was correct. However, because syllabus requirements change, you must **always** check with your examination group or your teacher before you start any coursework to make sure that you are doing what is required.

NB There is a requirement for coursework to involve primary data or fieldwork in several cases.

Examination groups: addresses

LEAG – London and East Anglian Group

London	University of London Schools Examinations Board Stewart House, 32 Russell Square, London WC1B 5DN
LREB	London Regional Examinations Board Lyon House, 104 Wandsworth High Street, London SW18 4LF
EAEB	East Anglian Examinations Board The Lindens, Lexden Road, Colchester, Essex CO3 3RL (0206 549595)

MEG – Midlands Examining Group

Cambridge	University of Cambridge Local Examinations Syndicate Syndicate Buildings, 1 Hills Road, Cambridge CB1 2EU (0223 61111)
O & C	Oxford and Cambridge Schools Examinations Board 10 Trumpington Street, Cambridge CB2 1QB and Elsfield Way, Oxford OX2 8EP
SUJB	Southern Universities' Joint Board for School Examinations Cotham Road, Bristol BS6 6DD
WMEB	West Midlands Examinations Board Norfolk House, Smallbrook Queensway, Birmingham B5 4NJ
EMREB	East Midland Regional Examinations Board Robins Wood House, Robins Wood Road, Aspley, Nottingham NG8 3NR

NEA – Northern Examination Association (*write to your local board.*)

JMB	Joint Matriculation Board (061-273 2565) Devas Street, Manchester M15 6EU (*also for centres outside the NEA area*)
ALSEB	Associated Lancashire Schools Examining Board 12 Harter Street, Manchester M1 6HL
NREB	North Regional Examinations Board Wheatfield Road, Westerhope, Newcastle upon Tyne NE5 5JZ
NWREB	North-West Regional Examinations Board Orbit House, Albert Street, Eccles, Manchester M30 0WL
YHREB	Yorkshire and Humberside Regional Examinations Board Harrogate Office — 31–33 Springfield Avenue, Harrogate HG1 2HW Sheffield Office — Scarsdale House, 136 Derbyshire Lane, Sheffield S8 8SE

NISEC – Northern Ireland

NISEC	Northern Ireland Schools Examinations Council Beechill House, 42 Beechill Road, Belfast BT8 4RS (0232 704666)

SEB – Scotland

SEB	Scottish Examinations Board Ironmills Road, Dalkeith, Midlothian EH22 1BR

SEG – Southern Examining Group

AEB	The Associated Examining Board Stag Hill House, Guildford, Surrey GU2 5XJ (0483 503123)
Oxford	Oxford Delegacy of Local Examinations Ewert Place, Summertown, Oxford OX2 7BZ
SREB	Southern Regional Examinations Board Eastleigh House, Market Street, Eastleigh, Hampshire SO5 4SW
SEREB	South-East Regional Examinations Board Beloe House, 2–10 Mount Ephraim Road, Tunbridge Wells TN1 1EU
SWEB	South-Western Examinations Board 23–29 Marsh Street, Bristol BS1 4BP

WJEC – Wales

WJEC	Welsh Joint Education Committee 245 Western Avenue, Cardiff CF5 2YX (0222 561231)

(The boards to which you should write are underlined in each case.)

INDEX